Gallery of American Quilts

of
American

1830-1991   BOOK 3

American Quilter's Society

P. O. Box 3290 • Paducah, KY 42002-3290

Notice

The quilts in this book are no longer for sale. They were offered by members of the American Quilters's Society in 1990 and 1991. Approximately 70% of these quilts sold. The rest were returned to the members.

A one-year *Quilts For Sale* catalog subscription is only $16.00 (item #3201) for 4 issues. Each catalog contains more than 130 full-color photographs of quilts for sale with descriptions and prices. A singe copy of the catalog is $5.00 (ask for the latest issue).

Still available from the American Quilter's Society is the second book from this Gallery series:

item #2129 – *Gallery of American Quilts 1860-1989 Book 2* $19.95

Add $1.00 postage for the first book and $.40 for each additional copy your order. Send check, money order or MasterCard/VISA information to:

American Quilter's Society
P.O. Box 3290
Paducah, KY 42002-3290

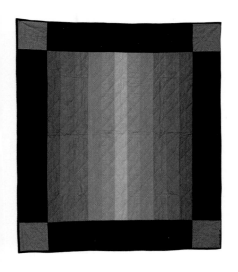

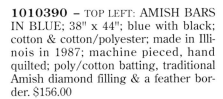

1010390 – TOP LEFT: AMISH BARS IN BLUE; 38" x 44"; blue with black; cotton & cotton/polyester; made in Illinois in 1987; machine pieced, hand quilted; poly/cotton batting, traditional Amish diamond filling & a feather border. $156.00

2010390 – TOP RIGHT: THE OUTDOORSMAN; 47" x 57"; navy, red & beige; cotton; made in Wisconsin in 1989; machine pieced & quilted, hand embroidered & appliqued; polyester fiberfill batting, blue backing. $173.00

3010390 – CENTER LEFT: SUPERNOVA; 35" x 35"; dusty blue & mauve; cotton/poly; made in Missouri in 1988; machine pieced, hand quilted; Mennonite made, signed & dated, Dacron batting. $92.00

4010390 – CENTER: "KOHOLA" – CORAL REEF; 52" x 32"; deep pine applique & binding, seafoam background; Imperial broadcloth; made in Marshall Islands in 1989; hand quilted & appliqued; designed & stitched in tra-

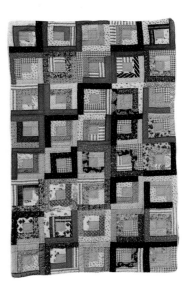

ditional Hawaiian manner with quilting ½" apart, machine wash & dry. $340.00

5010390 – CENTER RIGHT: LOG CABIN; 44" x 70"; multi-prints & natural muslin; muslin cotton & blend; made in Kentucky in 1988; hand pieced, hand quilted; lining is muslin, top is cotton & cotton blend with poly batting. $156.00

6010390 – BOTTOM LEFT: DOUBLE IRISH CHAIN; 50" x 50"; blue, muslin, rust/blue/brown print; cotton; made in North Carolina in 1984; machine pieced, hand quilted; polyester batting, light blue back, unused, quilted with light blue thread. $173.00

7010390 – BOTTOM RIGHT: FOUR OF HEARTS; 27½" x 27½"; rose/natural; cotton & blends; made in California in 1987; machine pieced, hand quilted, hand appliqued; four hearts in assorted rose tone fabrics appliqued in each square, rose print backing. $69.00

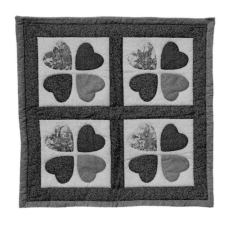

1020390 – TOP LEFT: PECK HOLE; 81" x 96"; scrap with muslin set up in pink; poly cotton blend; made in Ohio in 1983; machine pieced, hand quilted; polyester batting. $288.00

2020390 – TOP RIGHT: ALTERNATING BLOCK PATTERN; 77" x 96"; bright blue, red & green with matching plaid; top is wool blends, back is cotton flannel; made in Ohio in 1989; machine pieced, hand tied. $288.00

3020390 – CENTER LEFT: ZYGOCACTUS; 55" x 53"; off-white, dark green, shades of purple & mauve/pink; 100% cotton; made in Wisconsin in 1988; machine pieced, hand quilted; 100% polyester batting, heavily quilted. $196.00

4020390 – CENTER: OHIO STAR IMAGES I; 25" x 25"; tapestry of lilac, peach & ecru; 100% cotton, polyester batting; made in New Hampshire in 1989; machine pieced, hand quilted; unique octagonal shape. $87.00

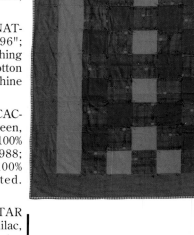

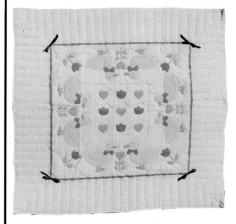

5020390 – CENTER RIGHT: DUCKS SHADOW; 40" x 40"; white with orange, yellow, green & teal; 100% cottons with top layer of voile; made in Colorado in 1987; hand quilted & appliqued; signed & dated. $115.00

6020390 – BOTTOM LEFT: SILVER BELL ANNIVERSARY; 16½" x 16½"; white; poly blend cotton; made in Texas in 1988; hand quilted, painted & embroidered; bells painted with metallic paint, touches of silver gray embroidery thread, edged with metallic lace, place for anniversary date to be added under bells. $35.00

7020390 – BOTTOM RIGHT: GRAB BAG STYLE; 82" x 84"; multi-colored, blues, brown & pink; cotton, cotton polyester; made in Washington in 1984; machine pieced, hand quilted; polyester batt. $345.00

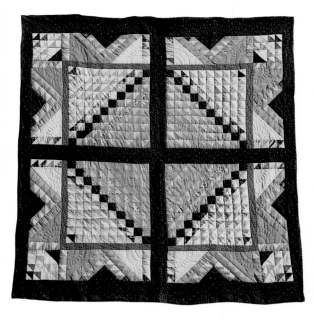

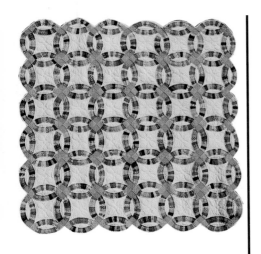

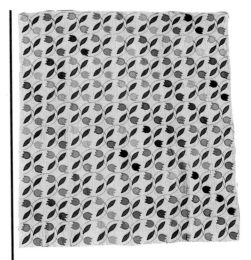

1030390 – TOP LEFT: DOUBLE WEDDING RING; 86" x 86"; multi-color prints with white; cotton/cotton blends; made in 1987; hand pieced & quilted; Mountain Mist batt. $489.00

2030390 – TOP RIGHT: TULIP; 86" x 93"; multi-colored tulips with green leaves & stems on white background; cotton blends; made in Tennessee in 1984; tulips & leaves are hand appliqued & stems are hand embroidered with 6 strands embroidery floss, squares are sewn by machine; hand quilted; polyester batting. $978.00

3030390 – CENTER RIGHT: BOW TIE; 78" x 90"; varied colors; cotton & cotton blends; made in Arkansas in 1988; hand & machine pieced, hand quilted; mixed prints & solids. $230.00

4030390 – CENTER: GRANDMOTHER'S FLOWER GARDEN; 72" x 96"; multi-color; cotton; made in Ohio in

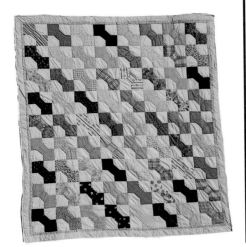

1980; hand pieced, hand quilted. $230.00

5030390 – CENTER RIGHT: ROYAL STAR OF ALABAMA; 91" x 100"; dark & light blue prints & solids; cotton-polyester blend; made in Missouri in 1989; machine pieced, hand quilted. $345.00

6030390 – BOTTOM LEFT: BASKETS/WITH CURRENTS; 78" x 85"; pink, blue, green on white; cotton, homespun; made in Pennsylvania c. 1830; hand pieced, hand quilted, hand appliqued; cotton batting with seeds, fine quilting & cording. $1,380.00

7030390 – BOTTOM RIGHT: SHOO FLY; 78" x 90"; blue & white; cotton; made in New Hampshire in 1987; machine pieced, hand quilted; poly batting. $575.00

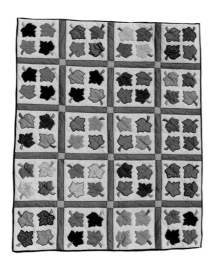

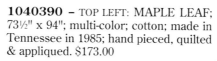

1040390 – TOP LEFT: MAPLE LEAF; 73½" x 94"; multi-color; cotton; made in Tennessee in 1985; hand pieced, quilted & appliqued. $173.00

2040390 – TOP RIGHT: SUNBURST; 90" x 104"; blue & white; cotton & polyester; made in Indiana in 1980; hand pieced & quilted; comes with 2 pillow shams, batting is polyester. $690.00

3040390 – CENTER LEFT: CAROLINA LILY; 80" x 94"; white & green with shades of pink; cotton; made in 1989; appliqued & machine pieced, hand quilted; polyester batting. $288.00

4040390 – CENTER: FLYING GEESE WALLHANGING; 29" x 29"; shades of maroon & pink; cotton; made in Illinois in 1988; machine pieced, hand quilted; patchwork blocks put together with fly-

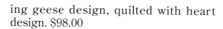

ing geese design, quilted with heart design. $98.00

5040390 – CENTER RIGHT: PYRAMID; 66" x 78"; variegated prints; cotton & poly blends; made in Kentucky in 1988; machine pieced & quilted; polyester batting, has green lining & orange binding with scalloped sides. $173.00

6040390 – BOTTOM LEFT: MONKEY WRENCH; 78" x 92"; blue & white; 100% pre-washed cotton; made in New York in 1989; machine pieced, hand tied, hand finished; blue print with solid navy squares, Mountain Mist polyester fill. $156.00

7040390 – BOTTOM RIGHT: ROCKY ROAD TO DURBIN; 86" x 88"; navy & white; pre-washed polyester & cotton; made in Kentucky in 1989; hand & machine pieced, hand quilted. $403.00

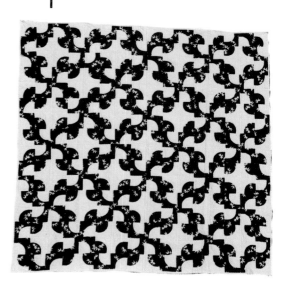

1050390 – TOP LEFT: FLOWER PATCH; 84" x 98"; white, greens, orange, yellow, blue & pink binding; made in 1986; hand pieced & quilted; Mountain Mist poly batt. $575.00

2050390 – TOP RIGHT: SPRING BLOSSOM; 87" x 98"; medium blue print, solid white & rose; broadcloth; made in Arkansas in 1989; hand pieced & quilted; border machine made, sheet backing, polyester batting, double binding. $242.00

3050390 – CENTER LEFT: HAYE'S CORNER; 80" x 92"; tan, red & black; 100% cotton; made in Pennsylvania in 1989; 100% polyester batting, back has pieced design of print & black blocks, alternate blocks have quilted feathered square, has rod pocket. $748.00

4050390 – CENTER: GRANDMOTHER'S FLOWER GARDEN; 67" x

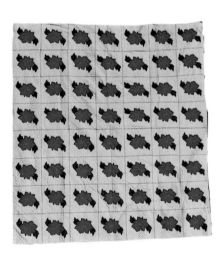

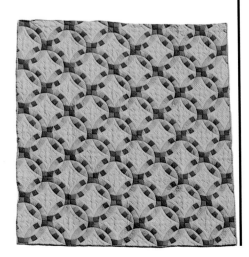

76"; multi-color; cotton; made in Tennessee in 1948; hand pieced & quilted; minor stain. $156.00

5050390 – CENTER RIGHT: POINSETTIA; 76" x 88"; red & green on white background; made in Tennessee in 1980; machine & hand quilted; hand appliqued with embroidery, squares & green stitching sewn by machine, Mountain Mist batt. $920.00

6050390 – BOTTOM LEFT: WEDDING RING; 86" x 91"; beige & mauve; polyester & cotton; made in Illinois in 1989; hand quilted; light blue back. $202.00

7050390 – BOTTOM RIGHT: STAR BOUQUET; 75" x 87"; varied prints & solids; cotton & cotton blends; made in Arkansas in 1989; hand pieced & quilted; muslin backing, double bias binding. $230.00

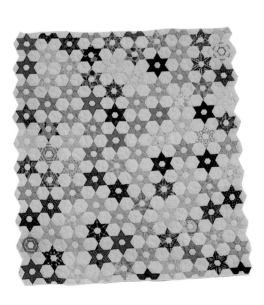

1060390 – TOP LEFT: AMISH-STYLE QUILT; 44" x 44"; black, 3 shades of blue; 100% cotton; made in California in 1989; machine pieced, hand quilted; 100% cotton batting, back is solid blue, signed & dated. $150.00

2060390 – TOP RIGHT: BUNNIES; 29" x 42"; pastel pink, blue, lavender & green on white; 100% cotton; made in Ohio in 1989; machine pieced & appliqued, hand & machine quilted; bunnies have white lace on collars, rod pocket for hanging, signed & dated, bonded polyester batting. $92.00

3060390 – CENTER LEFT: PAMANI-VMA KE KAI (Coco Palms By The Sea); 30" x 40"; brown & gold; cotton polyester; made in Hawaii in 1986; hand appliqued & quilted; polyester batting. $403.00

4060390 – CENTER: UNCLE SAM

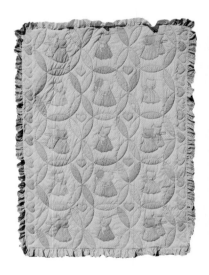

©Country Threads Pattern; 31" x 31"; red, navy, green & black; 100% cotton; made in New York in 1989; machine pieced, hand appliqued & quilted; poly batting, signed & dated. $144.00

5060390 – CENTER RIGHT: HEARTS & DOLLS; 46" x 62"; pink, white & blue; polyester/cotton; made in Pennsylvania in 1989; hand quilted; Dacron batting, white eyelet ruffle, quilted with pink embroidery thread. $144.00

6060390 – BOTTOM LEFT: PINEAP-PLE; 81" x 81"; navy, wine & assorted calicoes; top mostly cottons from 1940's; made in Delaware; hand pieced & quilted in 1989. $460.00

7060390 – BOTTOM RIGHT: LOVER'S KNOT; 77" x 96"; red & white; cotton blends; made in Kentucky in 1989; hand pieced & quilted; white lining is pre-washed sheet. $483.00

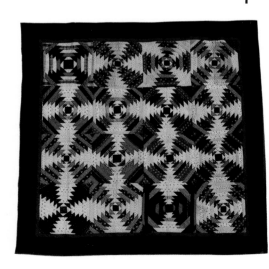

1070390 – TOP LEFT: POINSETTIA; 71" x 93½"; red, green, white & yellow; cotton & cotton/polyester; made in Wisconsin in 1988; machine pieced, hand quilted; polyester batt. $184.00

2070390 – TOP RIGHT: BROKEN STAR; 98" x 98"; multi-color; broadcloth top & bastiste bottom; made in Ohio in 1986; machine pieced, hand quilted; Mountain Mist Dacron batting, bright & colorful, solid colors in quilt top, quilted in some feather designs in the border & in some of large center blocks. $598.00

3070390 – CENTER RIGHT: TRUMPET VINE; 78" x 80"; red, green, orange calico with off-white background; cotton; made in Illinois c. 1880; hand pieced & quilted; cotton batting, some discoloring in background. $345.00

4070390 – CENTER: NORTH PIER LIGHTHOUSE; 41" x 44"; red, white, blue & black; cotton; made in Wiscon-

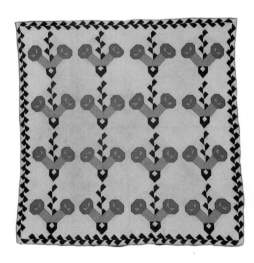

sin in 1989; hand appliqued & embroidered, machine stitched & quilted. $87.00

5070390 – CENTER RIGHT: VARIABLE STAR; 30" x 30"; red, grays & cream; pre-washed cotton; made in Massachusetts in 1989; machine pieced, hand quilted; polyester batting; has rod pocket. $98.00

6070390 – BOTTOM LEFT: MEXICAN ROSE; 86" x 105"; white background with forest green, dark orange, coral & gold; 100% cotton; made in Arizona in 1989; hand appliqued & quilted, machine stitched backing; background quilting ¾" apart, polyester batting. $690.00

7070390 – BOTTOM RIGHT: STAR OF GEORGIA; 77" x 91"; mauve & white; cotton blends; made in Kentucky in 1989; hand pieced & quilted; white lining is pre-washed sheet. $391.00

9

1080390 – TOP LEFT: STAR & CROSS; 83" x 99"; mauve & wine; cotton; made in California in 1989; machine pieced, hand quilted; Mountain Mist poly batting, double bias binding. $443.00

2080390 – TOP RIGHT: NECKTIE; 81" x 87"; multi-colored; cotton; made in Indiana; hand & machine pieced, hand quilted; polyester batting, primitive. $288.00

3080390 – CENTER LEFT: GORGEOUS POPPIES; 48" x 48"; green, red & off-white; cotton-polyester blend; made in Idaho in 1989; hand appliqued & quilted; Mountain Mist batting. $110.00

4080390 – CENTER: PUSS IN THE CORNER; 51" x 72½"; cotton; made in

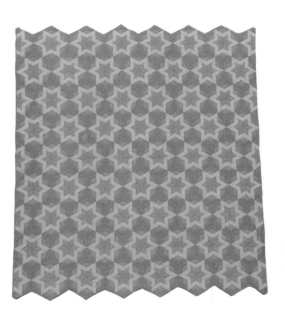

Illinois c. 1900; hand pieced & quilted; cotton batting, bound on 3 sides, top has been faced. $230.00

5080390 – CENTER RIGHT: STARS AND BLOCKS; 82" x 92"; blue; cotton; made in Illinois in 1989; machine pieced, hand quilted; made of 2 prints & 1 plain blue. $374.00

6080390 – BOTTOM LEFT: ENIGMA STAR; 75" x 91"; red, white & blue; 100% cotton; made in Maine in 1989; machine pieced, hand quilted; 100% cotton muslin back, polyester low loft batt; signed & dated. $357.00

7080390 – BOTTOM RIGHT: BASKET OF FLOWERS; 91" x 95"; blue, cranberry & rose; 100% cotton; made in Tennessee in 1989; hand appliqued & quilted; 1930's look with natural muslin background. $690.00

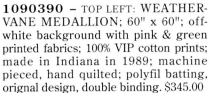

1090390 – TOP LEFT: WEATHER-VANE MEDALLION; 60" x 60"; off-white background with pink & green printed fabrics; 100% VIP cotton prints; made in Indiana in 1989; machine pieced, hand quilted; polyfil batting, orignal design, double binding. $345.00

2090390 – TOP RIGHT: EAGLE APPLIQUE; 78" x 94"; cream yellow on white background; cotton; made in Illinois c. 1930; hand appliqued with hand crochet edge; cotton batting, grid & outline quilted, small break in crochet on top, several breaks in grid quilting. $345.00

3090390 – CENTER LEFT: IRISH CHAIN (Variation); 72" x 84"; red & white; cotton; made in Pennsylvania c. 1920; machine pieced, hand quilted; cotton batting. $432.00

4090390 – CENTER: NANCY'S FANCY; 36" x 36"; pink, blue, gray &

white; cotton, cotton & polyester; made in Minnesota in 1986; hand pieced & quilted; pocket rod for hanging, polyester batting, machine washable. $144.00

5090390 – CENTER RIGHT: FOLDED STAR; 70" x 80"; scrap cottons; made in California in 1986; machine pieced, tied; 100% polyester batting. $144.00

6090390 – BOTTOM LEFT: LOG CABIN STAR; 86" x 102"; shades of blue with touch of pink; cotton with poly backing; made in Kansas in 1989; machine pieced, hand quilted; double binding, signed & dated. $483.00

7090390 – BOTTOM RIGHT: SIMPLE PLEASURES VARIATION; 77" x 97"; cream, brown & green; cotton & cotton blends; made in North Dakota in 1989; machine pieced & quilted; polyfil batting, signed & dated. $276.00

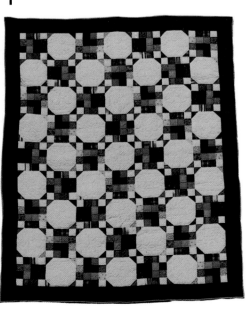

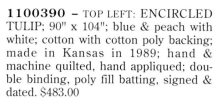

1100390 – TOP LEFT: ENCIRCLED TULIP; 90" x 104"; blue & peach with white; cotton with cotton poly backing; made in Kansas in 1989; hand & machine quilted, hand appliqued; double binding, poly fill batting, signed & dated. $483.00

2100390 – TOP RIGHT: GARDEN WEDDING; 84" x 106"; multi-color; cotton/polyester; made in Missouri in 1989; machine pieced, hand quilted; polyester batting. $345.00

3100390 – CENTER LEFT: POTTED CACTUS; 75" x 95"; green, beige, pink & yellow; cotton & cotton blend; made in Arkansas in 1988; hand & machine pieced, hand quilted; polyester batting, cotton blend backing. $230.00

4100390 – CENTER: GRAND-MOTHER'S FLOWER GARDEN II; 82" x 63"; multi-color prints & solids; cotton;

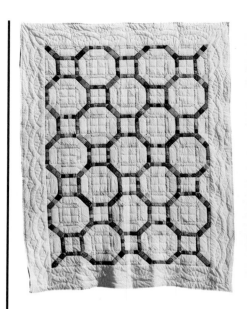

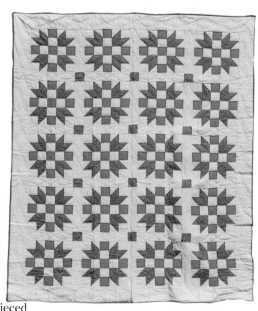

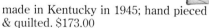

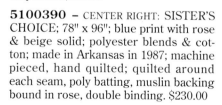

made in Kentucky in 1945; hand pieced & quilted. $173.00

5100390 – CENTER RIGHT: SISTER'S CHOICE; 78" x 96"; blue print with rose & beige solid; polyester blends & cotton; made in Arkansas in 1987; machine pieced, hand quilted; quilted around each seam, poly batting, muslin backing bound in rose, double binding. $230.00

6100390 – BOTTOM LEFT: HIDDEN SAMPLER; 86" x 86"; red & blue; cotton; made in California in 1989; machine pieced & quilted; polyester batting. $173.00

7100390 – BOTTOM RIGHT: REGENCY; 82" x 97"; earth tones; polyester & cotton; made in Kentucky in 1980; cross stitched, hand quilted; metallic thread running through center of flower & leaf, Mountain Mist 100% polyester batting. $460.00

1110390 – TOP LEFT: OHIO STAR; 90" x 105"; red, white & blue; cotton; made in Montana in 1987; machine pieced & quilted; polyester batting. $518.00

2110390 – TOP RIGHT: FEATHERED STAR; 90" x 102" ; navy & cream; cotton-poly mix; made in Oregon in 1989; machine pieced, hand quilted. $345.00

3110390 – CENTER LEFT: OHIO STAR; 76" x 86"; gold & white; cotton; made in Ohio in 1920's; hand pieced & quilted; mustard gold stars on white background. $328.00

4110390 – CENTER: FRIENDSHIP DAHLIA; 66" x 86"; multi-color with pink & turquoise sashing; cotton; made in Kansas in 1930's; hand appliqued & quilted; turquoise & pink fabrics are home-dyed feed sack, has names

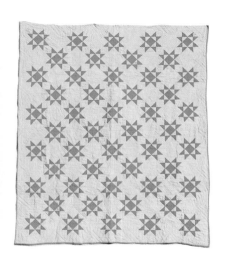

embroidered on flower stems, cotton batting, shows some use. $288.00

5110390 – CENTER RIGHT: LITTLE RED SCHOOL HOUSE; 72" x 87"; red, black & white; cotton; made in Georgia in 1989; hand pieced & quilted; white lining, polyester batting. $403.00

6110390 – BOTTOM LEFT: BLUE-BIRDS FOR HAPPINESS; 92" x 104"; blue print & solid, white, unbleached muslin; perma-press materials; made in California in 1989; blocks hand pieced, border & binding machine stitched, hand quilted; Dacron polyester batting. $489.00

7110390 – BOTTOM RIGHT: WILD GOOSE CHASE; 82" x 100"; blue & white; cotton; made in Kentucky in 1989; hand pieced & quilted; cross feather quilting design. $374.00

13

1120390 – TOP LEFT: VIENNA ROSE; 84" x 102"; beige, rust, brown & blue; cotton & cotton blend; made in Ohio in 1985; hand quilted & appliqued. $690.00

2120390 – TOP RIGHT: BROKEN STAR; 91" x 91"; shades of lavender; polyester & cotton; made in Illinois in 1988; machine pieced, hand quilted; polyester batting, signed & dated. $575.00

3120390 – CENTER LEFT: BROKEN GLASS; 74" x 92"; coral & light blue print; cotton & cotton blends; made in Louisiana in 1989; machine pieced, hand quilted. $288.00

4120390 – CENTER: ALTERNATING FOUR PATCH; 58" x 88"; chambray blues; 100% cotton; made in Illinois in 1989; machine pieced, hand quilted;

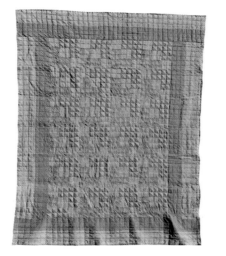

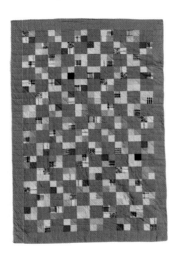

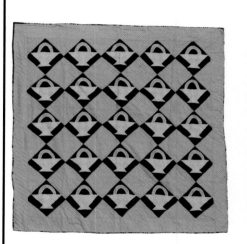

shirt plaids, prints & stripes with 100% cotton chambray, thin polyester batting. $259.00

5120390 – CENTER RIGHT: BASKETS; 78" x 78"; green, pale yellow & white; made in 1950; machine pieced, hand quilted; primitive. $230.00

6120390 – BOTTOM LEFT: SUN-FLOWER; 82" x 96"; multi-colored calico prints, light blue & white; 100% pre-washed cotton; made in Illinois in 1989; machine pieced, hand appliqued; Mountain Mist batting; light blue backing. $403.00

7120390 – BOTTOM RIGHT: BEAR'S PAW; 90" x 112"; ivory background with multi-color batik prints; made in Indonesia in 1989; machine pieced, hand quilted; polyester batting. $575.00

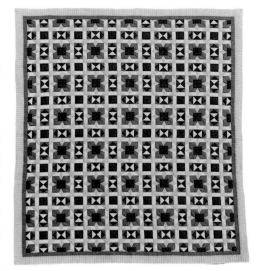

1130390 – TOP LEFT: OHIO STAR; 86" x 99"; light blue star with off-white background; cotton; made in Kentucky in 1989; hand pieced & quilted; cotton batting. $345.00

2130390 – TOP RIGHT: SUNBURST II; 84" x 96"; ivory, burgundy, dark & light seafoam green; polyester/cotton; made in 1989; hand pieced & quilted; Mountain Mist batting, ivory backing. $690.00

3130390 – CENTER LEFT: DOUBLE WEDDING RING; 81" x 106"; multicolor; cotton/polyester; made in Missouri in 1989; machine pieced, hand quilted; white fill, polyester batting. $345.00

4130390 – CENTER: LONE STAR; 84½" x 70½"; reds & blues; cotton; made in Tennessee in 1989; hand

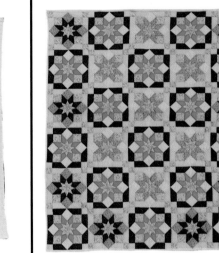

pieced & quilted; muslin background. $259.00

5130390 – CENTER RIGHT: STAR-BRIGHT; 76" x 88"; shades of blue, peach & orange; poly/cotton; made in Washington in 1989; hand pieced & quilted; poly batting. $345.00

6130390 – BOTTOM LEFT: L.S.U. TIGER; 81" x 94"; gold, purple; poly/cotton blends; made in Louisiana in 1989; machine pieced, hand quilted & appliqued; letters could be removed if needed, purple backing. $575.00

7130390 – BOTTOM RIGHT: LOG CABIN – SUNSHINE & SHADOWS; 49" x 49"; sage green & gray; 100% cotton; made in California in 1983; machine pieced & quilted; quilt-as-you-go method. $115.00

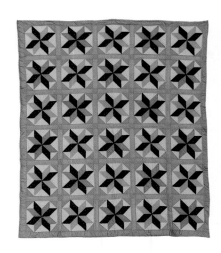

1140390 – TOP LEFT: UNKNOWN; 88" x 104"; stoneware blue/light & dark (dark blue side shown); 100% cotton; made in Idaho in 1988; hand quilted; reversible, polyester batting. $552.00

2140390 – TOP RIGHT: BARBARA FRIETCHIE'S STAR; 72" x 84"; lavender, blue, peach & green; cotton top; made in Arkansas in 1989; machine pieced, hand quilted; polyfil batting, back is tiny print with same colors as top, lavender bias binding, signed & dated. $230.00

3140390 – CENTER LEFT: CROWN OF THORNS; 84" x 100"; blues, cream; 100% pre-washed cotton; made in Illinois in 1989; machine pieced, hand quilted; dark blue sashing, Mountain Mist batting. $460.00

4140390 – CENTER: LONE STAR; 87" x 104"; mauves (solids & prints) with ecru background; poly/cotton; made in

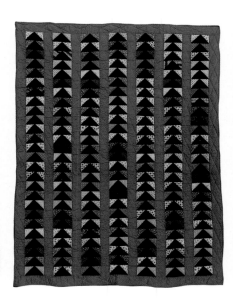

Ohio in 1989; machine pieced, hand quilted. $518.00

5140390 – CENTER RIGHT: WILD GOOSE CHASE; 76" x 101"; pink, black, multi-color prints; poly/cotton; made in Idaho in 1988; machine pieced, hand quilted. $374.00

6140390 – BOTTOM LEFT: BASKET OF FLOWERS; 88" x 100"; blues with multi-color flowers; cotton; made in Montana in 1988; hand quilted & painted, machine applique; poly batting, flower faces are hand painted. $489.00

7140390 – BOTTOM RIGHT: RIBBONS; 85" x 105"; forest greens, peaches (solids & prints); cotton & poly/cotton; made in 1989; machine pieced, hand quilted; polyester batting, hand bound with double fabric. $397.00

16

1150390 – TOP LEFT: DOVE AT SUN-RISE; 94" x 108"; pale blue blocks stripped with navy & orange; polyester & cotton; made in Arkansas in 1989; hand appliqued & quilted. $455.00

2150390 – TOP RIGHT: LONE STAR; 94" x 110"; shades of lilac on white; 100% cotton prints & polyester & cotton background; made in Missouri in 1989; machine pieced, hand quilted & bound, polyester batting. $403.00

3150390 – CENTER LEFT: DOUBLE WEDDING RING; 88" x 102"; multi-color on off-white; cotton; made in KY in 1989; hand quilted; Star lite Bonded Polyester Comfort Batting. $345.00

4150390 – CENTER: DRESDEN PLATE; 55" x 70"; greens & blues; cotton & cotton blends; made in MN in 1988; machine pieced & quilted, hand appliqued; muslin backing. $196.00

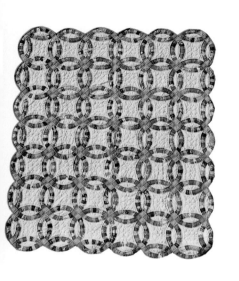

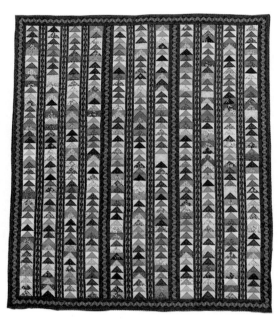

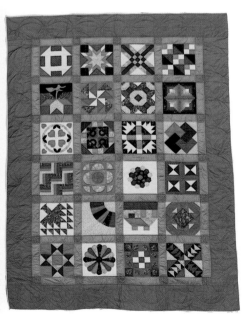

5150390 – CENTER RIGHT: FLYING GEESE; 96" x 104"; brown with mixed prints; 100% cotton; made in Arizona in 1986; machine pieced, hand quilted; signed & dated. $397.00

6150390 – BOTTOM LEFT: BLUE SAMPLER; 80" x 110"; blue prints & solids with white back; cotton blends; made in Arkansas in 1989; machine pieced, hand quilted; Fairfield Traditional batting, quilted by piece, quilted scallops on borders. $748.00

7150390 – BOTTOM RIGHT: ROMAN STRIPES; 85" x 100"; bold solids, black background; 100% pre-washed cotton; made in Illinois in 1989; machine pieced, hand quilted; Amish pattern, quilted with black thread & in the ditch, Mountain Mist batting. $483.00

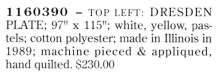

1160390 – TOP LEFT: DRESDEN PLATE; 97" x 115"; white, yellow, pastels; cotton polyester; made in Illinois in 1989; machine pieced & appliqued, hand quilted. $230.00

2160390 – TOP RIGHT: PRIMROSE BASKET; 85" x 105"; pinks, greens cream & gold; 100% cotton; made in Louisiana in 1989; machine pieced, hand quilted & appliqued; pre-washed fabrics, Mountain Mist Dacron batting, small double binding, off-white backing. $460.00

3160390 – CENTER LEFT: STARS IN STARS; 78" x 90"; light & dark blue on white; 100% pre-washed cotton; made in Illinois in 1989; machine pieced, hand quilted; Mountain Mist batting. $403.00

4160390 – CENTER: FAIRY TALE; 38" x 38"; maroon/navy/multi; cotton; made in Minnesota in 1989; hand quilted & appliqued. $46.00

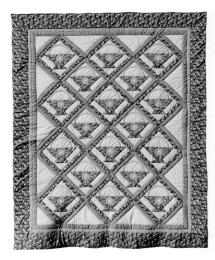

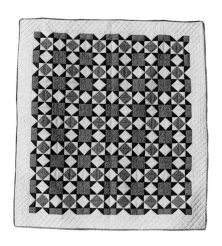

5160390 – CENTER RIGHT: RISING STAR; 85" x 103"; peach, mauve, burgundy print & burgundy on white background; cotton, cotton/poly; made in Michigan in 1989; machine pieced, hand quilted; polyester batting, signed & dated, heavily quilted with Prairie Point binding. $368.00

6160390 – BOTTOM LEFT: HAWAIIAN WATER LILY; 100" x 99"; light blue on dark blue; cotton; made in 1983; machine pieced, hand appliqued & quilted; 7 to 8 stitch per inch. $1,150.00

7160390 – BOTTOM RIGHT: GRAND-MOTHER'S FAN; 84" x 104"; blue with touch of pink; cotton with poly cotton lining; made in Kansas in 1989; machine pieced, hand quilted; polyester batting, double binding, mitered corners,each fan has nylon lace, signed & dated. $391.00

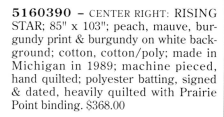

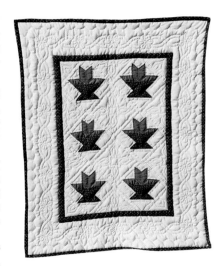

1170390 – TOP LEFT: LOG CABIN; 88" x 98"; browns & peaches; cotton blends; made in IL in 1987; machine pieced & quilted; bonded batting, light peach lining, w/pillows & wallhanging. $288.00

2170390 – TOP RIGHT: MINIATURE BASKET; 21" x 27"; off-white, white, brown, red & green; cotton poly; made in Illinois in 1989; machine pieced, hand quilted. $58.00

3170390 – CENTER LEFT: AMISH TRIPLE RAIL; 60" x 60"; black w/pink & blue; 100% cotton; made in Ohio in 1989; machine pieced, hand quilted; Mountain Mist Blue Ribbon 100% cotton batting, double binding, black backing. $288.00

4170390 – CENTER: HOMES OF LOVE; 33½" x 45"; cranberry, navy, off-white calicoes; 100% cotton; made in New Hampshire in 1989; machine pieced, hand quilted; backing is same fabric as border. $144.00

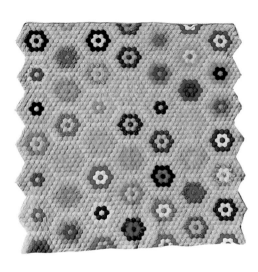

5170390 – CENTER RIGHT: FLOWER GARDEN; 100" x 100"; light rose w/multi-colored solids & prints; polyester cotton; made in 1987; machine pieced, hand quilted; polyester batting, muslin lining, w/matching pillow shams. $460.00

6170390 – BOTTOM LEFT: AMISH DIAMOND; 94" x 94"; red, blue, green & purple; pre-washed 100% cotton; made in Massachusetts in 1987; hand pieced & quilted; Mountain Mist poly batting, heavily quilted w/black, black back, needs cleaning. $518.00

7170390 – BOTTOM RIGHT: ANGEL'S FLIGHT; 83" x 102"; roses & blues; 100% cottons; made in Virginia in 1988; machine pieced, hand quilted; Highloft bonded poly fill, blue backing, double bound, signed & dated. $518.00

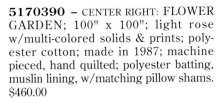

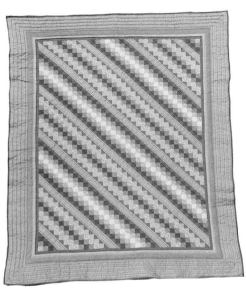

1180390 – TOP LEFT: TEXAS STAR; 108" x 110"; rose, mint green & white; all cotton; made in Alabama in 1985; machine pieced, hand quilted; quilted on each side of seam, white lining. $460.00

2180390 – TOP RIGHT: LOG CABIN; 84" x 97"; teal & pink; all cotton; made in Illinois in 1989; machine pieced & quilted; all cotton/poly batting, double binding, signed & dated, pieced block by block. $443.00

3180390 – CENTER LEFT: LOG CABIN FAN; 88" x 102"; shades of pink & rose with white; all cotton; made in Kansas in 1989; machine pieced, hand quilted; cotton poly backing, polyester batting, double binding, mitered corners, signed & dated. $460.00

4180390 – CENTER: OHIO STAR; 38" x 38"; country blue & rose; cotton/polyester blend; made in Kentucky in 1989;

hand & machine pieced, hand quilted; country blue calico pieced blocks & solid rose stars with a heart quilted in the center, bonded polyester batting. $189.00

5180390 – CENTER RIGHT: LOG CABIN; 42" x 56"; tones of blue, dusty mauve; cotton/poly; made in Illinois in 1989; machine pieced, hand quilted. $87.00

6180390 – BOTTOM LEFT: TRIP AROUND THE WORLD; 102" x 108"; turquoise & greens; all cotton; made in Oregon in 1989; machine pieced & quilted; Mountain Mist polyester batting. $357.00

7180390 – BOTTOM RIGHT: TRELLIS; 83½" x 95"; pastel pinks, blues, greens, yellow accent; 100% cotton; made in New York in 1989; machine pieced & quilted; Fairfield Traditional polyester batting, free-motion quilted. $460.00

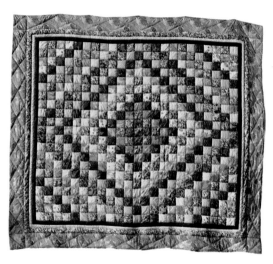

20

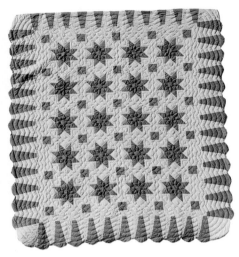

1190390 – TOP LEFT: STAR DAHLIA; 94" x 104"; country rose with country blue petals, off-white background; 100% cotton & polyester /cotton; made in Missouri in 1989; machine pieced, hand quilted; polyester batting. $374.00

2190390 – TOP RIGHT: RAIL FENCE; 92" x 110"; yellow, red & blue; cotton polyester; made in Illinois in 1989; machine pieced, hand quilted; reversible. $230.00

3190390 – CENTER LEFT: HEIR-LOOM; 90" x 108"; red, blue & off-white; cotton; made in Kentucky in 1984; hand pieced & quilted; Starlight bonded polyester batting. $345.00

4190390 – CENTER: MYOMI; 46½" x 62½"; red, black, gray with multi-color kimonos; 100% cotton & polyester; made in Maryland in 1989; hand & machine pieced, hand quilted; gray

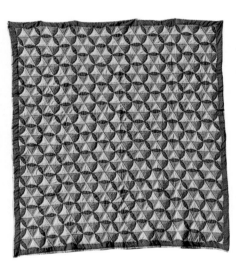

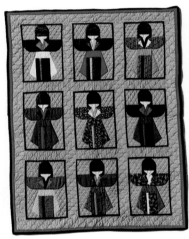

background, has pocket rod, 100% polyester batting, background quilted in diamond pattern, sashing & border quilted in shell pattern. $230.00

5190390 – CENTER RIGHT: BUTTER-FLY; 95" x 100"; off-white blocks stripped with orange & brown; polyester & cotton with poly-fil; made in Arkansas in 1989; hand quilted & appliqued. $518.00

6190390 – BOTTOM LEFT: COL-ORADO LOG CABIN; 82" x 102"; blue; cotton /polyester; made in Missouri in 1989; machine pieced, hand quilted; polyester batting. $403.00

7190390 – BOTTOM RIGHT: DRES-DEN PLATE; 42" x 42"; blue on white; cotton/poly; made in Illinois in 1989; machine pieced, hand appliqued & quilted. $127.00

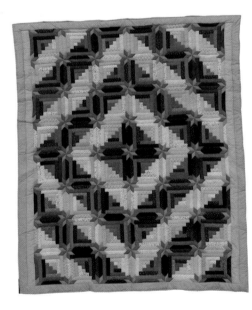

1010690

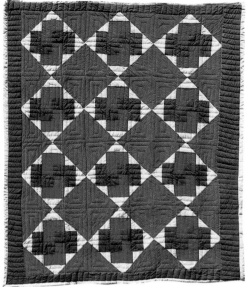

2010690

3010690

4010690

5010690

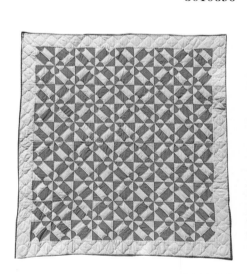

6010690

7010690

1010690 – AUTUMN SAMPLER; 62" x 94"; rust background with coordinating prints in all blocks; cotton & cotton blends; made in Arkansas in 1987; machine pieced & quilted; medium weight batting. $282.00

2010690 – BLOCKS; 80" x 94½"; red, white & blue; cotton; made in Georgia in 1989; hand pieced & quilted; set together with red, white & blue cotton print, white lining, polyester batting, quilted in blocks. $374.00

3010690 – CAROLINA LILY; 61" x 82"; red & green on white background; cotton; made c. 1900; machine pieced, hand appliqued & quilted; cotton batting, several red flowers have been replaced. $403.00

4010690 – VICTORIAN SKATER; 26" x 33"; blues, muslin & plum; cottons, velour & satin; made in Minnesota in 1987; machine pieced, appliqued & quilted; poly batting, snowflakes added. $90.00

5010690 – GIANT DAHLIA; 82" x 102"; peaches, light teal blues, white background; 100% cotton; made in Pennsylvania in 1990; machine pieced, hand quilted; Fairfield 100% bonded polyester batting, unbleached muslin backing, feather quilting all around, feathered hearts on pillow tuck, never used. $661.00

6010690 – UNKNOWN; 77" x 78"; orange & white; antique top is 100% cotton; quilted in Ohio in 1985; hand pieced & quilted; orange cotton/polyester backing, Mountain Mist 100% polyester batting. $345.00

7010690 – CATHEDRAL WINDOW; 80" x 96"; muslin & multi-colors; cotton & few blends; made in California in 1974; hand pieced; bright prints give look of stained glass, precision joins between blocks form tiny petal-shape folds. $1,495.00

1020690

2020690

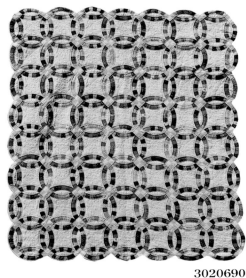

3020690

4020690

5020690

6020690

1020690 – VIRGINIA'S LOG CABIN; 78" x 93"; multi-color; cotton/polyester; made in Missouri in 1989; machine pieced, hand quilted; polyester batting. $345.00

2020690 – NORTH CAROLINA ROSE; 65" x 80"; lavender, green, brick red & cream; cotton; pieced in 1938, quilted in 1989 in Kentucky; hand pieced, appliqued, embroidered & quilted; signed & dated, polyester batting. $575.00

3020690 – DOUBLE WEDDING RING; 85" x 96"; white, small prints, white lining; cotton/poly-cotton blends; made in Arkansas in 1990; hand pieced & quilted; wedding bells quilted in each block, Fairfield Traditional Poly batting, signed & dated. $500.00

4020690 – PERSIAN JEWELS; 46" x 46"; teal, burgundy, rose & tan; cotton & chintz; made in Minnesota in 1990; machine pieced, hand quilted; polyester batting. $228.00

5020690 – MAINE SAMPLER; 80" x 95"; pink, brown, burgundy & white; calico fabrics; made in Missouri in 1989; machine pieced, hand quilted & appliqued; feather quilting, cross hatching in border, pieced ribbon border, calico print backing & polyester batting. $460.00

6020690 – TRIP AROUND THE WORLD; 82" x 98"; dark green, sea foam green, rust, peach, off-white; 100% cotton; made in Indiana in 1989; machine pieced, hand quilted; poly batt, pre-washed, dark green border with accented edging of same fabrics in top. $431.00

7020690 – RIBBONS & BOWS; 62" x 80"; pink, sea foam green & blue; 100% cotton Concord fabrics; made in Illinois in 1990; machine pieced, hand quilted; delicate ribbons breeze through color-coordinated fabrics, Blue Ribbon Cotton Classic batting, 100% cotton unbleached muslin backing. $431.00

7020690

1030690

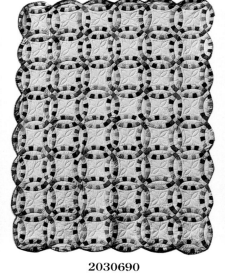

2030690

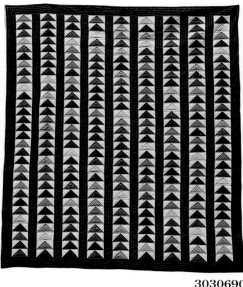

3030690

4030690

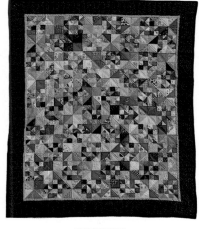

5030690

6030690

7030690

1030690 – EIGHT POINTED STARS; 79" x 93"; blue & tan; 100% cottons; made in Virginia in 1989; machine pieced, hand quilted; pre-washed fabrics, pieced lattice work, traditional bonded poly batting, double bound edges, mitered corners, intricate border design in quilting, signed & dated, reversible. $460.00

2030690 – DOUBLE WEDDING RING; 80" x 106"; blue prints with white background; cotton/polyester; made in Missouri in 1989; machine pieced, hand quilted; polyester batting. $345.00

3030690 – FLYING GEESE; 83" x 95"; shades of green; cotton/poly blend; made in Arkansas in 1989; machine pieced; Fairfield Traditional batting, seamless white 50/50 backing, prints in shades of green & joined with bands of delicate vine striped designer fabric in dark green, mitered corners, signed & dated. $546.00

4030690 – THE UNICYCLE; 48" x 48"; red, lavender, aqua, yellow & white; cotton; made in Massachusetts in 1987; machine pieced, hand quilted; cotton flannel batting, some strip piecing, very light, hanging sleeve attached. $460.00

5030690 – FOUR SQUARE; 72" x 84"; multi-color; cotton; hand pieced & quilted. $431.00

6030690 – LOG CABIN VARIATION; 82" x 82"; gray/green logs with blue center, cream & black border; 100% cotton; made in Bermuda in 1989; machine pieced, hand quilted; fiddle head fern quilting design, polyester batting. $431.00

7030690 – LONE STAR; 85" x 106"; pink print with white background; cotton; made in Kentucky in 1989; machine pieced, hand quilted; cotton batting. $374.00

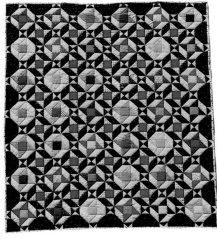

1040690

2040690

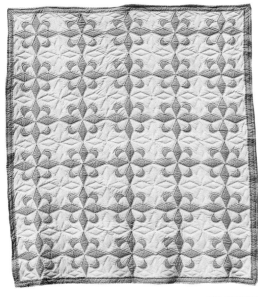

3040690

4040690

5040690

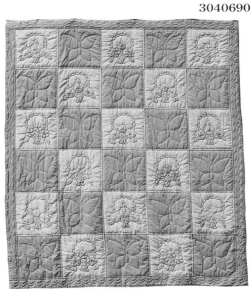

6040690

1040690 – BLUEGRASS FESTIVAL; 60" x 68"; multi-primary on black & white with coordinated back; cotton & cotton/poly; made in Washington in 1990; hand pieced & quilted; poly-bonded batting. $259.00

2040690 – DELECTABLE SUNRISE; 50" x 50"; cream, tan, brick red print with tan & cream pattern; cotton, cotton blend; made in Connecticut in 1990; machine pieced, hand quilted; poly-fil batting. $144.00

3040690 – STAR AND CRESENT; 78" x 90"; lavender print on white background; cotton broadcloth & print; made in Tennessee in 1989; hand pieced & quilted; lavender stripe lining, polyester batting. $345.00

4040690 – PIECED HEART; 33" x 49"; shades of blue, very light brown background print; 100% cotton; made in Wisconsin in 1990; machine pieced, hand quilted; polyester batting, hearts quilted into background with dark blue thread. $196.00

5040690 – MONKEY WRENCH; 72" x 85"; assortment of prints with brown & dark gold; all cotton; made in Ohio; hand pieced & quilted; fabrics date back to 1880's, cotton batting. $518.00

6040690 – EMBROIDERED BASKETS OF FLOWERS; 80" x 108"; blue & white embroidered in all colors of flowers; all cotton/poly sheets; made in Missouri in 1989; machine pieced, hand quilted; brown basket filled with flowers, dusty blue set up, never used. $196.00

7040690 – LOG CABIN; 90" x 102"; blue on blue; cotton; made in Alabama in 1990; machine pieced, hand quilted; sheet lining, poly batting, quilted on each side of seam. $403.00

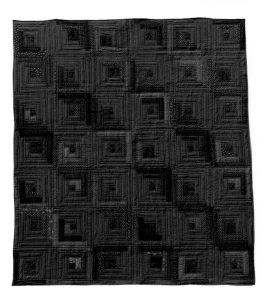

7040690

1050690

2050690

3050690

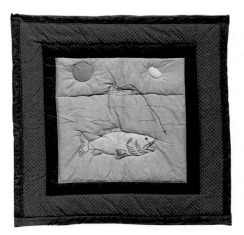

4050690

5050690

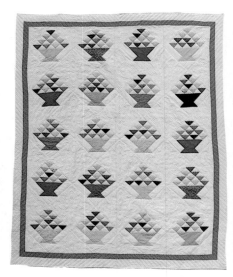

6050690

7050690

1050690 – PAUL REVERE QUILT; 72" x 72"; white, brown, red, blue & gold; 100% cotton solids; made in Florida in 1987; hand pieced & quilted; Cotton Classic batting, silhouette of Paul Revere, quilted landscape with details, pieced border of Minutemen & British soldiers. $1,150.00

2050690 – TREE OF LIFE; 74" x 85"; pink, rose & burgundy flowers, green leaves, white background; cotton; made in Nebraska in 1930's; hand appliqued & quilted, embroidered details on flowers & leaves; white background, 4 bouquets in corners, embroidered flowers around outside border, scalloped borders, some yellowing from age. $748.00

3050690 – COLORADO LOG CABIN; 78" x 100"; mixed; cotton; made in Arkansas in 1989; machine pieced, hand quilted; cotton muslin back, polyfil batting, hand bound with 100% cotton handmade bias, pre-washed fabrics, signed & dated. $345.00

4050690 – FISHING; 40" x 40"; light green, dark green, red multi; cotton & cotton polyester; made in Wisconsin in 1990; machine pieced & quilted, hand appliqued & embroidered; poly cotton bonded batting. $86.00

5050690 – OCEAN WAVES VARIATION; 82" x 96"; black, gray, pink pattern, salmon, over dyed; 100% cotton; made in Utah in 1988; machine pieced, hand quilted; 100% polyester batting, fabrics were hand over-dyed, quilted in pink. $978.00

6050690 – BASKET; 80" x 102"; multi-color; cotton; made in Kentucky in 1989; hand pieced & quilted. $345.00

7050690 – OHIO STAR; 88" x 112"; light green, rose & white; cotton muslin & calico; made in Illinois in 1989; hand & machine pieced, hand quilted; Mountain Mist 100% Polyester batting, white muslin backing. $725.00

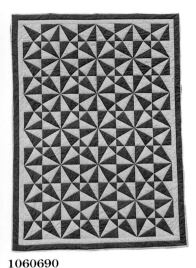

1060690

2060690

3060690

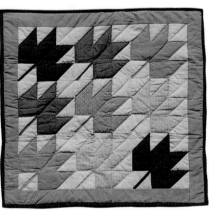

4060690

5060690

6060690

1060690 – CROSSED CANOES; 65" x 91"; blue & white; cotton; made in Colorado in 1990; machine pieced & quilted; Mountain Mist Polyester batting, signed & dated. $443.00

2060690 – BLUE ON BLUE SAMPLER; 86" x 95"; Williamsburg blue; 100% cotton; made in North Carolina in 1988; machine pieced, hand quilted; traditional batting, lap quilted method. $633.00

3060690 – LOG CABIN/STRAIGHT FURROW; 67" x 88"; multi-color with red centers; cottons & blends; made in Massachusetts in 1990; machine pieced, hand quilted; fleece batting, muslin backing. $288.00

4060690 – MAPLE LEAF; 28½" x 28½"; peach & golden browns; 100% cotton; made in California in 1988; machine pieced, hand quilted; poly batting, muslin backing with fabric loops for hanging, signed. $69.00

5060690 – CRAZY QUILT; 86" x 88"; browns & colors of 1930 period with pink as dominant color; cotton; made in Midwest in 1930's; hand pieced & quilted; cotton batting, country look, back is dark green calico print, border is brown calico print. $403.00

6060690 – HAWKS AND GEESE; 76" x 88"; blue, tan, cranberry, mauve & off-white; 100% cotton; made in Maine in 1989; machine pieced, hand quilted; flower print background & border, intricate circular design quilted in center with rest being diagonal quilting, single piece muslin back, Mountain Mist Quilt Light batting, signed & dated. $345.00

7060690 – TRUE LOVER'S KNOT; 66" x 100"; teal, cream, rose & prints; 100% cotton; made in Michigan in 1989; machine pieced, hand quilted; Fairfield Traditional batting. $431.00

7060690

1070690

2070690

3070690

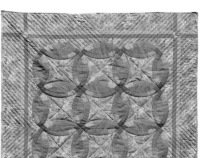

4070690

5070690

6070690

7070690

1070690 – GRANDMOTHER'S FLOWER GARDEN; 90" x 107"; red prints & solids; cotton with muslin path between flowers; made in Virginia in 1989; machine pieced, hand quilted; muslin backing, polyester batting. $518.00

2070690 – DOUBLE IRISH CHAIN; 78" x 98½"; lavender prints, pastel green; 100% cotton; made in New York in 1989; machine pieced & quilted; white floral background, Mountain Mist Polyester batting, machine washable. $403.00

3070690 – AMISH BARS; 96" x 96"; dark gray, black, purples, olive, turquoise & beige; 100% cotton; made in Massachusetts in 1988; machine pieced, hand quilted; heavily quilted in Cable & Pumpkin Seed patterns with black thread, black back with handmade bias binding, Mountain Mist poly batting, signed & dated. $518.00

4070690 – DOUBLE WEDDING RING WALLHANGING; 48" x 57½"; shades of dusty pinks; 100% cotton; made in Iowa in 1989; machine pieced & quilted, hand appliqued; Mountain Mist Low Loft batting, 4" hanging sleeve. $230.00

5070690 – DRESDEN PLATE; 88" x 104"; slate blue & rose; cotton; made in Kansas in 1989; machine pieced, hand quilted; mitered corners, double binding, polyfil batting, signed & dated. $449.00

6070690 – DRUNKARD'S PATH; 78" x 92"; hunter green solid on rust & white mini-print background; cotton, poly-cotton; made in New York in 1983; machine pieced, hand quilted; Dacron batting, never used. $399.00

7070690 – FLYFOOT or CATCH ME IF YOU CAN; 75" x 84"; medium blue & white; all cotton; made in Ohio c. 1930; hand pieced & quilted; cotton batting, few age spots in one corner. $305.00

1080690

2080690

3080690

4080690

5080690

6080690

7080690

1080690 – CIRCLES & STARS; 76" x 88"; multi-color with off-white solid lining; cotton; made in Mississippi in 1989; machine pieced, hand quilted; Polyester Fluff batting. $230.00

2080690 – COLONIAL LADY; 72" x 89"; blue & matching blue print; polyester & cotton; made in Indiana in 1988; hand appliqued, machine quilted; sleeve for hanging, pre-washed. $150.00

3080690 – COLONIAL LADY; 78" x 104"; mixed color with muslin background; cotton prints & solids; made in 1975; hand appliqued, hand quilted; Mountain Mist Polyester batting, back is white batiste. $431.00

4080690 – BLUE TULIP; 35" x 35"; blue, navy & off-white; cotton, cotton & polyester; made in Minnesota in 1989; hand pieced, appliqued & quilted; polyester batting, heavily quilted with feather sprays in large off-white spaces, has hanging sleeve. $109.00

5080690 – TUMBLING BLOCKS; 89" x 104"; country & navy blues & prints; cotton & poly cotton; made in Kansas in 1985; machine pieced, hand appliqued & quilted; 3-D effect, polyfil batting, signed & dated, center background is off-white, never used. $437.00

6080690 – CAROLINA LILY; 68" x 101"; pink, green; 100% cotton; made in California in 1989; machine pieced, hand appliqued & quilted; black background, pink flowers & baskets, green accents, floral border, sculptured bias border, polyester batting, French bias binding, signed & dated. $1,150.00

7080690 – COUNTRY STRING QUILT; 54" x 82"; multi-color; cotton; made in Kansas c. 1930's; machine pieced, hand quilted; muslin backing, cotton batting, lightweight quilt. $230.00

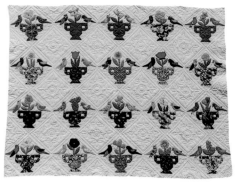

1090690

2090690

3090690

4090690

5090690

6090690

7090690

1090690 – GARDEN BOUQUET; 62" x 74"; multi-print blocks; cotton; made in Missouri in 1930's; hand pieced & appliqued, set together by machine & hand quilted; lightweight poly batting, unusual pattern. $460.00

2090690 – LONE STAR; 72" x 82"; multi-color; cotton; made in Montana & South Dakota in 1988; machine pieced, hand quilted; polyester batting, very colorful, creme accents & backing. $374.00

3090690 – PEACH HEART QUILT; 60" x 78"; peach, green & white; 100% cotton; made in Pennsylvania in 1990; machine pieced; Mosaic Piecing technique, polyester batting. $184.00

4090690 – OCEAN WAVE VARIATION; 34½" x 34½"; black & 18 traditional Amish colors; 100% cotton; made in Michigan in 1990; machine pieced, hand quilted; pre-washed, Mountain Mist batting, hanging sleeve, outline quilting, hearts with stems & leaves on border. $196.00

5090690 – MOOD INDIGO; 90" x 113½"; light to dark blues; all cotton; made in Iowa in 1989; machine pieced, hand quilted; light blue print backing, binding is variegated to match pattern of quilt, Lowloft polyfil batting, signed & dated. $690.00

6090690 – LOVE APPLE VARIATION; 83" x 85"; green, red & gold; cotton; made in Virginia c. 1860; hand pieced, appliqued & quilted; white background, cotton batting with leaf debris apparent when held to light, closely quilted, some uneven fading of green. $1,150.00

7090690 – LAUREL; 72" x 90"; shades of lemon & orange with brown; polyester blends; made in 1986; hand appliqued, hand quilted; 100% polyester batting, never used. $345.00

30

1100690

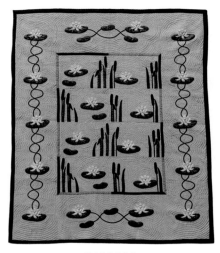

2100690

3100690

4100690

5100690

6100690

1100690 – TRIP AROUND THE WORLD; 69" x 86"; various prints & solids; cotton & cotton blends; made in Kentucky in 1989; hand pieced, machine quilted; polyester batting. $201.00

2100690 – WATER LILIES; 78" x 94"; light pink, dark green & brown; cotton & cotton velveteen; made in Montana in 1985; hand appliqued, painted & quilted; Mountain Mist Regular batting, hanging sleeve, cattails are stuffed, lily pads lightly stuffed, center of lily pads are outline stitched, has echo quilting. $1,035.00.00

3100690 – STRING; 65" x 45"; multi-colored; made in Texas in 1990; machine pieced, hand quilted; poly/cotton batting, made of 216 different men's neckties, green & black border. $230.00

4100690 – STAR BOUQUET; 89" x 95"; multi-color; cotton & cotton blends; made in Arkansas in 1989; hand pieced & quilted; double bias binding. $259.00

5100690 – BRICK WALK; 42" x 49"; multi-colored; cotton, cotton-polyester; made in Pennsylvania in 1988; machine pieced, hand quilted; polyester batting, background triangles are off-white prints, black & brown striped borders, gray backing. $316.00

6100690 – BEAR'S PAW; 76" x 86"; red, blue & off-white; cotton; made in Illinois in 1989; machine pieced, hand quilted; polyester batting. $276.00

7100690 – HEXAGONS; 72" x 87"; browns, tans, light gold; cotton & cotton polyester blends; made in New Jersey in 1986; machine pieced, hand quilted; bonded polyester batting. $518.00

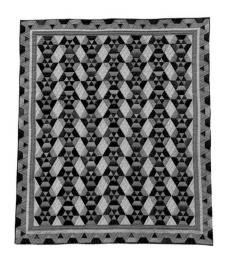

7100690

1110690

2110690

3110690

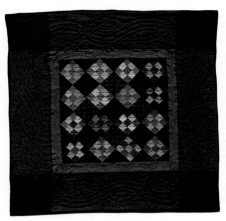

4110690

5110690

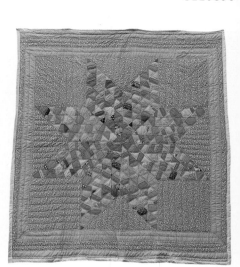

6110690

7110690

1110690 – DRUNKARD'S PATH; 85" x 110"; purple & cream; cotton & blends; made in Arkansas in 1989; hand & machine pieced, hand quilted; polyester batting, quilted around seams, double binding. $230.00

2110690 – FRIENDSHIP PLUME; 74" x 96"; blue & ivory; cotton & blend; made in Ohio in 1988; hand pieced & quilted; old Mountain Mist pattern. $575.00

3110690 – LOG CABIN; 70" x 96½"; reds; cotton; made in Tennessee in 1989; machine pieced, hand quilted; polyester batting. $288.00

4110690 – 9-PATCH RAINBOW; 31½" x 31½"; multi on black; cottons; made in North Dakota in 1989; machine pieced, hand quilted; blue borders, green corners, Amish nine patch set on point, sleeve for hanging, signed & dated. $115.00

5110690 – CRAZY PATCH; 74" x 84"; variety of prints, solids, checks, plaids, etc.; cottons & cotton poly blends; made in Kentucky in 1988; machine pieced & quilted; polyester batting, soft gray lining. $201.00

6110690 – LONE STAR; 71" x 78½"; mainly pinks; cotton; made in Tennessee in 1940's; hand pieced & quilted; polyester batting. $230.00

7110690 – DRUNKARD'S PATH; 78" x 92"; green & yellow; all cotton; made in North Carolina in 1930's; machine pieced, hand quilted; yellow lining, thin cotton batting. $575.00

1120690

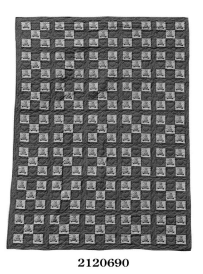

2120690

3120690

4120690

5120690

6120690

1120690 – CONSTELLATION; 92" x 110"; navy, lavender, orange & yellow; polyester-cotton blends; made in Illinois in 1987; hand pieced & quilted; contemporary medallion quilt using hexagons, diamonds & triangles; polyester batting, signed & dated. $575.00

2120690 – BEARHEARTS; 67" x 91"; gray & rust; cotton & cotton blend; made in Nebraska in 1989; machine pieced, hand quilted; polyester batting, background & borders are rust, teddies are gray & rust on white, bears are outline quilted, hearts quilted in plain blocks, signed & dated. $299.00

3120690 – ROBBING PETER TO PAY PAUL; 62" x 84"; blue & white; 100% cotton; made in Massachusetts in 1984; hand pieced & quilted; Mountain Mist polyester batting. $345.00

4120690 – FLOWER DESIGN; 80" x 96"; slate blue; cotton & poly; made in Pennsylvania in 1990; hand quilted; reversible/white, 100% Dacron poly batting. $575.00

5120690 – PERIWINKLE, A HAWAIIAN STYLE QUILT; 32½" x 32½"; blue with burgundy accent; cotton; made in Illinois in 1988; hand appliqued & quilted; polyester batting. $431.00

6120690 – DAHLIA; 44" x 44"; cream, coral & blue; 100% cotton; made in Indiana in 1989; machine pieced, hand quilted; poly batting, coral print backing, hanging sleeve. $104.00

7120690 – STAR; 35" x 35"; pink, green, yellow pastels; cotton; made in 1986; machine pieced, hand quilted; white background. $115.00

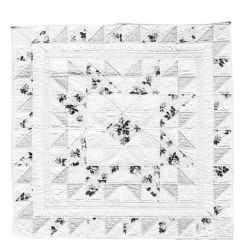

7120690

1130690

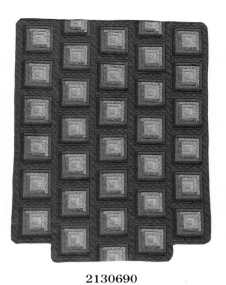

2130690

3130690

4130690

5130690

6130690

7130690

1130690 – BETHLEHEM STAR; 121" x 120"; yellows, greens & orange; cotton & poly blend; made in Kansas in 1985; machine pieced, hand quilted; soft yellow background, bias bound, double material for both 7 & 10" ruffles. $1,466.00

2130690 – LOG CABIN GARDEN STEPS; 85" x 107"; rust & blue; cotton & cotton poly; made in New Mexico in 1987; machine pieced & quilted; Mountain Mist batting. $345.00

3130690 – FEATHERED STAR; 89" x 100"; black, white & gray; poly-cotton; made in Oregon in 1990; machine pieced, hand quilted; made from Marsha McCloskey pattern. $345.00

4130690 – GIANT DAHLIA; 60" round; pinks & greens; cotton; made in Florida in 1988; machine pieced, hand quilted; pink backing & binding, Mountain Mist batting, signed & dated. $316.00

5130690 – BASKET SAMPLER; 46½" x 66"; blues, roses, mauves; 100% cottons & little blends; center block was winning entry in 1987 contest; quilt finished 1989 in New York; machine pieced, hand appliqued, embroidered & quilted; thin poly batting, signed & dated. $201.00

6130690 – PINWHEEL; 91" x 106"; rust & off-white; cotton/poly; made in Illinois in 1989; machine pieced, hand quilted; edges finished with prairie points. $397.00

7130690 – IRISH TULIPS; 82" x 101"; mauve, green & print fabricon white background; 100% cotton; made in Wisconsin in 1989; hand & machine pieced, hand quilted; quilted with prairie points. $529.00

34

1140690

2140690

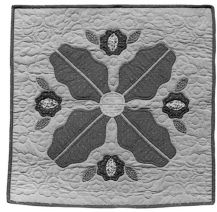

3140690

4140690

5140690

6140690

1140690 – LONE STAR; 114" x 101"; sea foam green, peach, brown, yellow & gold on white background; cotton/polyester blends; made in Virginia in 1974; machine pieced, hand quilted; polyester batting, Star portion quilted on both sides of seam, cable quilted wide borders & rounded pieced borders, signed & dated. $403.00

2140690 – LITTLE BITS; 36" x 50"; burgundy, gray, cream & pink; cotton/cotton blends; made in Alaska in 1989; machine pieced, hand quilted; Mountain Mist Polyester batting, black accents, back is unbleached muslin with tiny white print. $201.00

3140690 – A BAYOU DANCE; 27" x 27"; prints of red, blue, green & yellow; 100% cotton; made in Louisiana in 1990; hand appliqued & quilted; ecru background, red binding. $132.00

4140690 – PLAIN HAND QUILTED REVERSIBLE; 96" x 114"; unbleached muslin; cotton polyester; made in Illinois in 1989; hand quilted; light green points, reversible. $230.00

5140690 – SUNBONNET SUE; 24" x 24"; pink & blue; 100% cottons; made in Colorado in 1989; machine pieced, hand appliqued & quilted; sawtooth border. $115.00

6140690 – HAZY DISTRACTIONS; 43" x 53"; cobalt blue, earth tones & gray; cotton & cotton blends; made in Pennsylvania in 1989; machine pieced, hand quilted. $190.00

7140690 – CHECKERBOARD; 44" x 53"; muslin & multi prints; cottons & blends; made in North Carolina in 1990; machine pieced & quilted; thin polyester batting, vibrant colors. $104.00

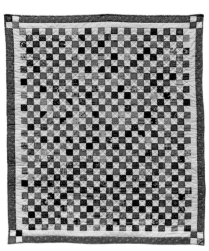

7140690

1150690

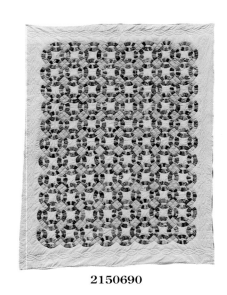

2150690

3150690

4150690

5150690

6150690

7150690

1150690 – DAHLIA; 96" x 109"; mauve; cotton/poly; made in Missouri in 1990; machine pieced, hand quilted; Dacron batting, made by Mennonites, signed & dated. $437.00

2150690 – WEDDING RING; 80" x 106"; multi-colors; cotton/polyester prints & solids; made in Iowa in 1988; hand pieced & quilted; Mountain Mist Polyester batting, white background. $345.00

3150690 – OHIO ROSE; 76" x 96"; mauve, rose & dark rose; cotton & poly cotton; made in Mississippi in 1990; hand pieced, appliqued & quilted; Extra-loft Polyfil batting. $575.00

4150690 – PRIMARY COLORS SAMPLER; 43" x 43"; royal blue, red & yellow; 100% cotton; made in New Hampshire in 1990; machine pieced, tied; thick polyester batting. $86.00

5150690 – MOUNTAIN MIST COUNTERPANE; 86" x 105"; white; cotton/poly; made in Michigan in 1983; hand quilted; Mountain Mist batting, never used. $835.00

6150690 – JACOB'S FAN; 84" x 106"; blue; cotton/polyester; made in Missouri in 1989; machine pieced, hand quilted; polyester batting. $345.00

7150690 – BUTTERFLY CROSS-STITCH; 93" x 115"; soft blue & white; cotton/poly; made in Illinois in 1989; finished edge with Prairie Points, white backing with shadow print & small blue & red flowers. $431.00

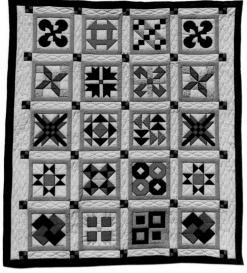

1160690

2160690

3160690

4160690

5160690

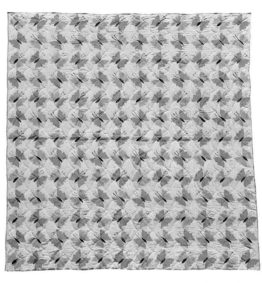

6160690

1160690 – CARDINAL POINT SAMPLER; 86" x 98"; red & navy blue; cotton/polyester; made in Missouri in 1990; machine pieced, hand quilted; polyester batting. $345.00

2160690 – DOUBLE PEONIES AND WILD ROSES; 88" x 109"; rose, blue, green & off-white; 100% cotton; made in Ohio in 1989; hand appliqued & quilted; polyester batting, alternate plain blocks quilted with 2 patterns, circular feathers & large bow with 3 flowers & stems, hand bound with double fabric, pre-washed fabric. $550.00

3160690 – APPLIQUED FLOWER; 85" x 101"; brown, beige & gold; poly blend cotton; made in Wisconsin in 1985; hand appliqued & quilted; heavy fiber fill batting. $460.00

4160690 – AUTUMN LEAVES; 81" x 97"; yellow, green, tan, brown & orange; cotton; made in Missouri in 1989; cross stitched, machine quilted; thin layer of cotton batting with cotton backing, dark orange binding around quilt, washable. $288.00

5160690 – JACOB'S ELEVATOR; 82" x 105"; country blue, mauve print; 100% pre-washed cotton; made in Illinois in 1990; machine pieced, hand quilted; Mountain Mist batting, country blue accent. $460.00

6160690 – BUTTERFLIES; 92" x 100"; dusty rose & blue; cotton percale; made in South Dakota in 1989; machine appliqued & quilted; Dacron batting, washable, butterflies on white block with alternate blue block. $345.00

7160690 – U.S. FLAG HOSTAGE QUILT; 108" x 118"; red, white & blue with gold trim; cotton blends; made in Washington in 1980; hand embroidered & quilted; Mountain Mist batting, washable, very detailed. $1,478.00

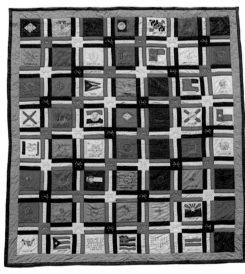

7160690

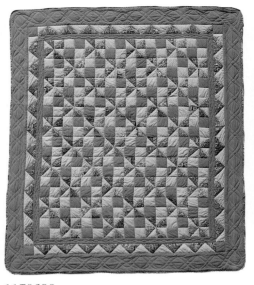

1170690

2170690

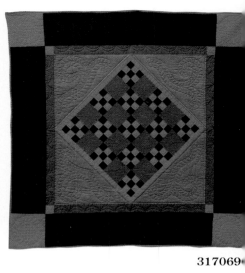

317069

4170690

5170690

617069

7170690

1170690 – WINDMILL; 84" x 95"; blue & white; cotton; made in Oregon in 1988; machin
pieced & quilted; Mountain Mist Fatt batting. $230.00

2170690 – OHIO STAR; 87" x 98"; green & wine on beige; 100% cotton; made in Arizona i
1989; machine pieced, hand quilted; pre-washed, signed & dated. $431.00

3170690 – AMISH-TYPE QUILT; 52" x 52"; black, teal, red & purple; 100% cotton; made i
Minnesota in 1984; polyester batting, quilted in white thread with feathers swags & bow designs
signed & dated. $288.00

4170690 – RUBIC'S STAR; 62" x 62"; 5 shades of reds, blues & greens on black; Broadclot
poly/cotton; made in Pennsylvania in 1988; machine pieced, hand quilted; poly fill 100% polyeste
$345.00

5170690 – CATHEDRAL WINDOWS; 41" x 78"; multi-color; cotton; made in Illinois in 1987
hand pieced; each "window" backed with filling giving a puffed look. $173.00

6170690 – SAMPLER; 81" x 96"; red & white; 100% cotton; made in California in 1980's
machine pieced, tied; 30 sampler blocks set together with lattice & cornerstones. $288.00

7170690 – CROWN OF THORNS; 79" x 101"; country blue & pink; 100% cotton; made in Nev
York in 1990; machine pieced, hand tied & finished; Mountain Mist polyester filling. $184.00

38

1180690

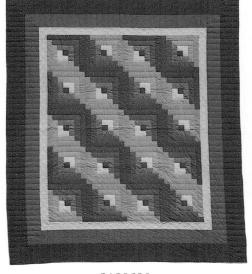

2180690

3180690

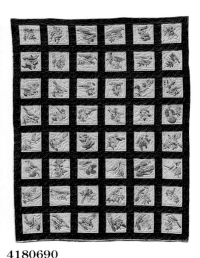

4180690

5180690

6180690

1180690 – LOG CABIN-BARN RAISING WITH A STAR; 90" x 106"; brown & tan calicoes; poly/cotton; made in Ohio in 1989; machine pieced, hand quilted; polyester batting. $397.00

2180690 – LOG CABIN; 82" x 96"; rust & yellow; cotton; made in Illinois in 1988; machine pieced, hand quilted; yellow check backing, double binding, has pillow, polyester batting, signed & dated. $547.00

3180690 – NIGHT & NOON VARIATION; 52" x 52"; darks of blue, purple, magenta, teal, painted surfaces of pearlized silver, gold, lavender, rose, champagne, blue prints; 100% cotton; made in Texas in 1987; machine pieced, hand & machine quilted; Cotton Classic batting. $1,783.00

4180690 – STATE BIRDS; 69" x 94"; white & dark green; cotton & cotton blend; blocks hand painted when only 48 U.S. states; hand quilted in Missouri in 1985; lightweight quilt. $288.00

5180690 – FAN; 82" x 96"; various prints; cotton/poly; made in Missouri in 1990; machine pieced, hand quilted; light green background, white lining. $345.00

6180690 – SUNFLOWER X-STITCH; 81" x 90"; yellow with green; cotton & cotton/poly blend; made in New Hampshire in 1987; hand quilted; white background, bonded poly batting. $460.00

7180690 – CARPENTER'S WHEEL; 40" x 40"; dark blue, cream, rust & light blue print; cotton & poly/cotton blend; made in California in 1990; machine pieced, hand quilted. $230.00

7180690

1190690

2190690

3190690

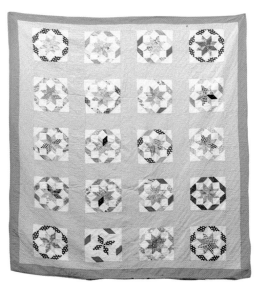

4190690

5190690

6190690

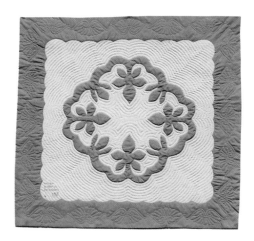

7190690

1190690 – BANBURY CROSS; 74" x 96"; cranberry, pinks, greens; all cotton; made in Pennsylvania in 1986; hand pieced & quilted; pink print backing, pre-washed. $345.00

2190690 – UNKNOWN; 84" x 104"; earth tones, brown, rust, beige & yellow; cotton & cotton/polyester; made in Indiana in 1989; hand appliqued & quilted; used pre-printed center, polyester batting. $437.00

3190690 – LONE STAR; 84" x 96"; tones of red & white; cotton; made in Canada in 1988; hand quilted; red lining, polyester batting. $575.00

4190690 – STAR IN A RING; 68" x 76"; multi; cottons; made in New York in late 1930's; hand pieced & quilted; yellow sashes & pink borders, soft lightweight quilt, some wear on binding. $230.00

5190690 – 9-PATCH; 33" x 38"; yellow & white; cotton & cotton/poly blend; made in Illinois in 1988; machine pieced, hand quilted; poly batting, initialed & dated. $63.00

6190690 – SAMPLER WALLHANGING; 32½" x 32½"; dusty rose & off-white; cotton; made in 1990; machine pieced, hand quilted; solid rose backing, binding is dark print of same colors. $75.00

7190690 – NOHO KAI - DWELLER ON THE SEASHORE; 34" x 34"; sky blue, ocean blue; cotton/poly; made in Marshall Islands in 1989; hand quilted & appliqued; sky blue background, designed & stitched in Hawaiian quilting manner, washable. $213.00

1010990

2010990

3010990

4010990

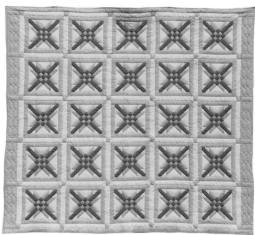

5010990

6010990

7010990

1010990 – PONTIAC STAR; 90" x 110"; red & white on white background; 50% cotton & 50% polyester; made in Iowa & Missouri in 1989; top is machine sewn, hand quilted; Mountain Mist batting. $391.00

2010990 – FLOWERS & BIRDS; 43" x 53"; pink printed design with flowers, birds & butterflies, white background, solid pink & white border; cotton, some blend; made in North Carolina in 1989; machine pieced, hand quilted; polyester batting; center design pink flowers, birds & butterflies, green leaves, center panel is pre-printed. $144.00

3010990 – TEXAS STAR; 72" x 84"; gray, maroon & rose; poly-cotton; made in Louisiana in 1990; hand pieced & quilted; African-American made quilt showing the Lone or Texas Star combined with the traditional African-American strip-pieced borders & quilting designs, polyester batting. $190.00

4010990 – STAR WITHIN A STAR; 89" x 98"; dark peach, rust & off-white; cotton & polyester blends; made in Illinois in 1988; machine pieced & quilted; VIP prints, binding is doubled & double stitched, polyester bonded batting. $173.00

5010990 – MEXICAN STAR; 89" x 96"; blue; cotton/polyester; made in Missouri in 1990; hand pieced & quilted; polyester fill. $345.00

6010990 – SHEEP; 77" x 94"; blue plaids, royal blue, red, tan; 100% cotton, some homespuns; made in New York in 1989; machine pieced, hand appliqued & quilted; poly batting, rail fence in border, heavy quilted, fabrics pre-washed. $403.00

7010990 – CANDLEWICKED SQUARES; 83" x 104"; off-white & brown; cotton; made in Pennsylvania & California in 1989; hand embroidered, machine pieced, hand quilted; bonded polyester batting, candlewicked squares, 3 borders of floral print, plain brown, floral print, quilted in concentric diamond pattern in sashing & border, brown border feather quilted. $834.00

41

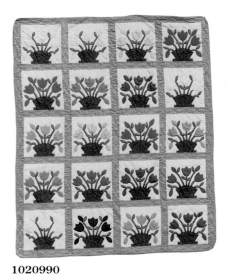

1020990

2020990

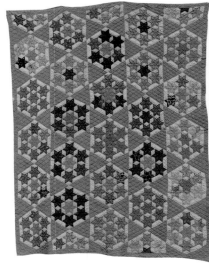

3020990

4020990

5020990

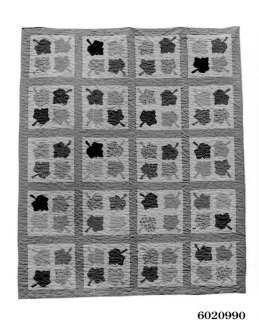

6020990

1020990 – A GARDEN OF TULIPS; 86" x 108"; multi-colors; cotton & cotton polyester; made in 1989; hand quilted & appliqued; no 2 blocks alike, sheet lining, poly fill. $460.00

2020990 – GRANDMOTHER'S FAN; 84" x 104"; shades of rose on cream background; all cotton; made in Kansas in 1989; machine pieced & hand quilted; mitered corners, double binding, poly fill batting, each block trimmed in lace, signed & dated. $483.00

3020990 – SEVEN SISTERS; 62" x 78"; print stars on off-white blocks with antique pink background; 100% cotton; made in Kentucky circa 1800's; hand pieced & quilted; thin cotton batting, heavily quilted, 1 small hole in top near edge. $403.00

4020990 – TWINKLE LITTLE STAR; 85" x 101"; multi-colored stars; cotton-polyester blend; made in Missouri in 1990; machine pieced, hand quilted. $403.00

5020990 – COLONIAL WILLIAMSBURG IN VIRGINIA; 78½" x 98½"; pastel blues & greens, dark green; poly/cotton & cotton; made in Minnesota in 1990; hand pieced, appliqued, embroidered & quilted; poly batting, original design. $1,725.00

6020990 – MAPLE LEAF; 80" x 100"; print leaves, white background with green sashing & binding; cotton & cotton/polyester; made in Indiana in 1988; hand appliqued, machine quilted; Mountain Mist batting, pre-washed. $144.00

7020990 – STAR & WREATH; 90" x 108"; blues; perma press cotton top & lining; made in Missouri in 1989; hand pieced & quilted; polyester batting, close to 300 hours by hand. $575.00

7020990

42

1030990

2030990

3030990

4030990

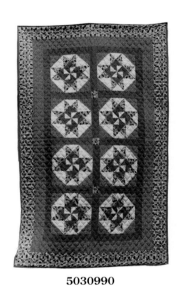

5030990

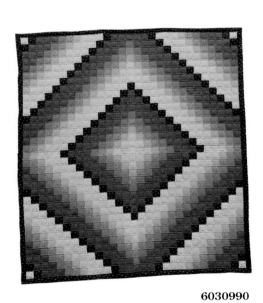

6030990

7030990

1030990 – TULIP; 73" x 91"; medium blue, rose & light blue on white background; cotton/poly blend; made in Arkansas in 1988; hand pieced & quilted; double bias binding, small stitches, polyester batting. $259.00

2030990 – DRESDEN PLATE; 72" x 83"; multi-colors with green sashing & binding on off-white background; 100% cotton; made in Bermuda in 1989; machine pieced, hand & machine appliqued, hand quilted; poly-cotton batting; has 20" matching cushion cover. $460.00

3030990 – SPRING FLOWERS; 82" x 98"; white background with peach, green, brown & orange; muslin; made in Illinois in 1987; hand embroidered & quilted; Hobbs extra fluffy batting. $380.00

4030990 – PINWHEEL VARIATION; 69" x 84"; tans & browns with blue, pink, red, & yellow accents; cottons, cotton/poly blend; made in Colorado in 1990; machine pieced, hand & machine quilted; Mountain Mist Poly batting, variation of Pinwheel pattern to give light & dark areas, signed & dated. $472.00

5030990 – PINWHEEL STAR; 60" x 98"; earth tones; cotton/polyester; made in Missouri in 1990; machine pieced & quilted; polyester batting. $144.00

6030990 – SUNSHINE & SHADOW; 90" x 102"; shades of gold & brown; cotton & cotton blends; made in Kansas in 1982; machine pieced, hand quilted; quilted ¼" inside each seam, polyester bonded batting, gold backing. $460.00

7030990 – DOUBLE WEDDING RING; 74" x 96"; red & black; 100% cotton; made in Massachusetts in 1986; hand pieced & quilted; pre-washed, dark red print on dark red background with black insets, quilted with dark red thread, hand made bias binding, heavily quilted with outline & flower & leaf designs, Mountain Mist batting, signed & dated. $460.00

43

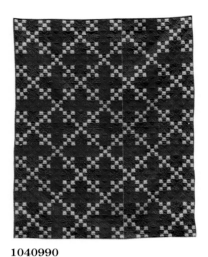

1040990

2040990

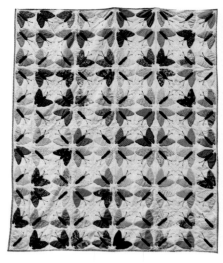

3040990

4040990

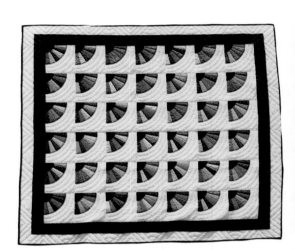

5040990

6040990

1040990 – ANTIQUE DOUBLE NINE PATCH; 56" x 71"; cranberry, white, black & white calicoes; cotton; maker of top unknown; hand quilted in early 1980's; excellent hand quilting. $575.00

2040990 – ROSE GARDEN; 68" x 86"; soft wedgwood rose & green; cotton & blends; made in Connecticut in 1989; machine pieced, tied; polyester batting. $253.00

3040990 – APPLIQUE BUTTERFLY; 80" x 96"; print butterflies on unbleached muslin background; 100% cotton; made in Arkansas in 1990; hand appliqued, embroidered & quilted; polyester bonded batting, pre-washed, each butterfly is different, handmade bias binding in butterfly print. $460.00

4040990 – DOGWOOD; 105" x 105"; rose & green; all cotton front with cotton poly backing; made in Kansas in 1990; machine pieced, hand quilted; poly fill batting, mitered corners, double binding, yellow centers lightly padded, signed & dated. $483.00

5040990 – TRANSIENT WORLD; 39" x 65"; blue, gray & cinnamon; cotton & blends; made in Pennsylvania in 1989; machine pieced, hand quilted; poly fiber batting. $202.00

6040990 – GRANDMA'S FAN; 88" x 98"; white & black with multi-color prints; cotton blend; made in 1990; machine pieced, hand quilted & appliqued; Mountain Mist batting. $317.00

7040990 – TUMBLIN' STAR; 97" x 97"; blue on blue; all cotton; made in Alabama in 1990; machine pieced, hand quilted; sheet lining, rose binding, quilted on each side of seam, poly batting. $374.00

7040990

1050990

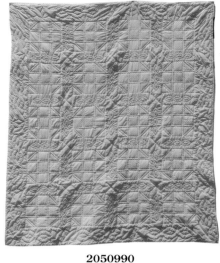

2050990

3050990

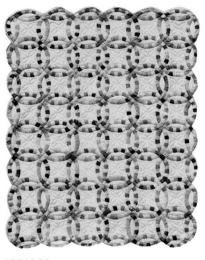

4050990

5050990

6050990

7050990

1050990 – NOSEGAY; 78" x 96"; multi-colored prints & solids; cotton & blends; made in Arkansas in 1988; machine pieced, hand quilted; polyester batting, muslin backing, light blue border with diamonds quilted in it, double bias binding. $230.00

2050990 – SHOO FLY; 83" x 98"; yellow & white; cotton & cotton/polyester; made in Montana & South Dakota in 1988; machine pieced, hand quilted; polyester bonded batting, muslin backing & binding, blocks are pale yellow print & white with light yellow border. $403.00

3050990 – CHARM; 80" x 88"; multi-colored print; cotton; made in Tennessee in 1989; hand pieced & quilted; beige sheet lining, polyester batting. $230.00

4050990 – DOUBLE WEDDING RING; 82" x 105"; multi-colored with white background; cotton/polyester; made in Missouri in 1990; machine pieced, hand quilted; polyester batting. $345.00

5050990 – TUNNEL OF LOVE; 77" x 85"; pink, mauve, aqua & off-white; cotton blends; made in Nebraska in 1989; machine pieced & quilted; polyfil batting, reversible, zigzag quilting. $190.00

6050990 – GIANT DAHLIA; 90" x 106"; sandy beige, brown & peach; cotton, cotton/poly; made in Michigan in 1989; machine pieced, hand quilted; polyester batting, dahlia is shades of brown with coral; white backing; outline quilted. $299.00

7050990 – SOLID RAIN HANDQUILTED; 91" x 106"; unbleached muslin, rose; cotton, poly-cotton; made in Illinois in 1990; hand quilted; solid color on each side, corners turned to show back. $230.00

45

1060990

2060990

3060990

4060990

5060990

6060990

1060990 – BEATRIX POTTER BABY QUILT; 38" x 52"; white background with blue sashing; cotton & cotton/poly blend; made in Oregon in 1990; machine appliqued & pieced; polyester fill, six characters from famous children's classics are appliqued, border & back of quilt feature more animals. $50.00

2060990 – SUPERNOVAE; 96" x 96"; blues, pinks, lavender & white; cotton calicoes; made in Nevada in 1990; machine pieced, hand quilted; Hobbs Poly-down batting, quilted by the patch, ¼" inside each piece. $460.00

3060990 – AMERICAN HERITAGE SAMPLER; 76" x 92"; white with blues, green & pinks; cotton; made in Montana in 1984; embroidery, cross-stitch, hand quilted; polyester batting. $690.00

4060990 – RAIL FENCE; 104" x 108"; black, rose, wine & cream; all cotton; made in Oregon in 1990; machine pieced & quilted; Mountain Mist polyester batting. $374.00

5060990 – LONE STAR; 101" x 116"; navy floral with tan & brick red; 100% pre-shrunk cotton; made in Indiana in 1989; machine pieced, hand quilted; 100% polyester batting, star is set on point with mitered borders & contains four different companion florals in rounds 5 & 6, corner blocks & binding. $1,035.00

6060990 – SCHOOL HOUSE; 80" x 98"; blue & white; cotton & cotton blend; made in Kentucky in 1989; hand pieced & quilted. $345.00

7060990 – HEARTS & SQUARES; 80" x 98"; multi-color; cotton; made in Illinois in 1989; machine pieced, hand appliqued & quilted; polyester batting, hearts are padded & set on off-white cotton. $288.00

7060990

1070990

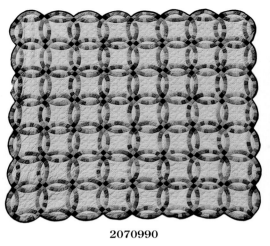

2070990

3070990

4070990

5070990

6070990

7070990

1070990 – FLOCK OF GEESE/OCEAN WAVES VARIATION; 54" x 66"; dark blue & natural; all cotton blue & white prints & muslin; made in Iowa in 1990; machine pieced, hand quilted; Poly low-loft batting, backing is cotton homespun, double bias binding. $207.00

2070990 – WEDDING RING; 90" x 92"; garden colors; cotton; made in Kentucky in 1989; machine pieced, hand quilted. $374.00

3070990 – PADDED DAISY; 92" x 108"; dusty blue & dusty rose; cotton/poly; made in Illinois in 1989; hand appliqued & quilted; padded flowers with machine embroidery outline the blocks, Dacron batting. $345.00

4070990 – TULIPS; 78" x 98"; white, red & green; 100% cotton; made in Wisconsin in 1989; hand appliqued & quilted. $437.00

5070990 – UNKNOWN; 90" x 102"; country sand; poly satin top with poly/cotton back; made in Pennsylvania in 1984; hand quilted; Dacron/Poly batting, reversible, eyelet ruffle with satin trim. $748.00

6070990 – PENNSYLVANIA DUTCH; 84" x 105"; multi-colored; muslin & polyester cotton; made in Nebraska in 1989; hand appliqued & quilted; Polyfil batting, muslin top with earthtone fabrics in applique. $690.00

7070990 – OHIO STAR; 87" x 102"; blue & pink print; 100% cotton; made in California in 1990; machine pieced, hand quilted; bonded polyester batting, cream background. $690.00

1080990

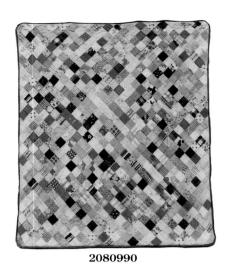

2080990

3080990

4080990

5080990

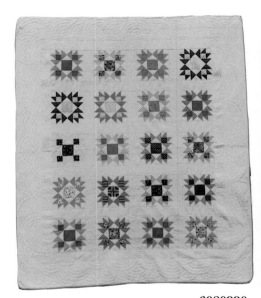

6080990

1080990 – VARIABLE STARS; 62" x 82"; blue, beige & rust; 100% cotton; made in New Hampshire in 1990; machine pieced, hand tied; double binding, hand embroidered label, Mountain Mist batting, fabric purchased in 1950's, alternating colors in stars, pre-washed fabrics. $259.00

2080990 – COBBLESTONES; 72" x 84"; variegated prints; cottons & cotton blends; made in Kentucky in 1989; hand pieced, machine quilted; polyester batting, off-white lining. $173.00

3080990 – GIANT DAHLIA; 64" x 91"; mauve & blues with off-white background; cotton, cotton blend; made in Nebraska in 1989; machine pieced, hand appliqued & quilted; Bonded Polyfil batting, hand sewn binding, borders hang over sides of bed, signed & dated. $374.00

4080990 – UNKNOWN; 76" x 96"; green; cotton & cotton polyester; made in Idaho in 1989; machine pieced, hand embroidered & quilted; Dacron-Poly batting, embroidered blocks. $345.00

5080990 – UNKNOWN; 85½" x 96½"; multi-colors set together with rose & aqua; cotton; made in Tennessee in 1940; hand pieced & quilted; primitive with some stains, collectible. $259.00

6080990 – VARIABLE STAR; 86" x 102"; scrap prints & soft shades of pink, coral, browns, greens & off-white; cottons, poly-cottons; made in New Hampshire in 1987; machine pieced, hand quilted; sashes have braids & borders, Mountain Mist batting, stars float on off-white background & blend with print back. $690.00

7080990 – LOG CABIN/BARN RAISING STYLE; 90" x 107"; country blue florals; poly/cotton; made in Ohio in 1989; machine pieced, hand quilted; polyester batting. $391.00

7080990

1090990

2090990

3090990

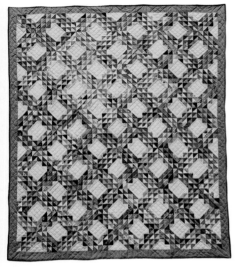

4090990

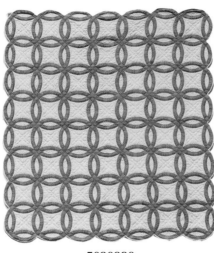

5090990

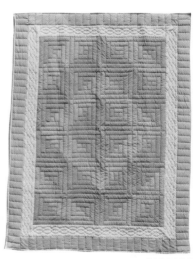

6090990

7090990

1090990 – LOG CABIN; 84" x 100"; multi-colors; 100% cotton top & lining; made in Alabama in 1990; machine pieced & quilted; polyester batting. $575.00

2090990 – DAHLIA; 70" x 102"; mauve, dusty pink; cotton/poly; made in Missouri in 1990; machine pieced, hand quilted; off-white background, Dacron batting, Mennonite-made, signed & dated. $317.00

3090990 – DOUBLE IRISH CHAIN VARIATION; 82" x 102"; rust & brown with white background; cotton; made in California in 1989; machine pieced, hand quilted; Mountain Mist Poly batting, double bias binding, pre-washed fabrics, quilted ¼" from seam method rather than on diagonal. $397.00

4090990 – OCEAN WAVES; 88" x 105"; peach with brown border; poly-cotton; made in Oregon in 1989; machine pieced, hand quilted; Fairfield batting. $345.00

5090990 – DOUBLE WEDDING RING; 84" x 96"; blue; cotton & polyester; made in Kentucky; hand pieced & quilted; backing is white 50% polyester & 50% cotton; 100% polyester batting. $432.00

6090990 – LOG CABIN; 73" x 102"; pink/peach; cotton/polyester; made in Missouri in 1990; hand pieced & quilted; polyester batting, includes matching wallhanging (38" x 38"). $403.00

7090990 – BUTTERFLY CHARM QUILT; 61" x 76"; multi-colored butterflies appliqued to unbleached muslin; cottons; made in Kansas in 1930's; hand appliqued & quilted; backing is floral, each butterfly from different fabric. $345.00

1100990

2100990

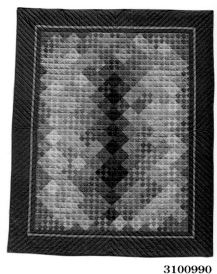

3100990

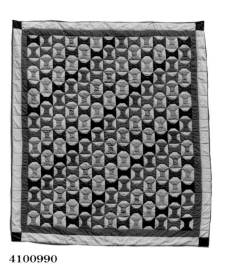

4100990

5100990

6100990

1100990 – STRING STAR; 60½" x 81"; multi-colors on off-white muslin background; cotton; top made in Tennessee in 1938; hand pieced & quilted; few age spots, blue border with pink block in each corner, polyester batting, older top newly quilted with new border. $345.00

2100990 – RINGS OF FLOWERS; 90" x 108"; pink & white with blue, green & pink floral circles; cotton; made in Virginia in 1988; hand embroidered, machine pieced & hand quilted; cotton/polyester batting. $460.00

3100990 – AM I BLUE (9 Patch); 74" x 93"; country blue prints with some beige & off-white; 100% cotton; made in Iowa in 1989; machine pieced, hand quilted; Poly batting, approx. 60 different prints used, backing is dark blue Jinny Byer blue on blue print, washable. $978.00

4100990 – SPOOLS; 72" x 84"; solid navy, red, gold, green, purple & blue spools set in cream solid background; cotton/poly blends & 100% cottons; made in Virginia in 1980's; machine pieced, hand quilted; double edge binding, muslin backing, Bonded Poly batting. $288.00

5100990 – IMPROVED 9-PATCH; 60" x 76"; navy blue & white; cotton; hand & machine pieced, hand quilted; older top, newly bound & quilted; pencil & pen marks on quilting lines. $374.00

6100990 – FLORAL ARRAY; 83" x 104"; soft pastels, rose, blue, green & off-white; 100% cotton; made in Ohio in 1990; hand appliqued & quilted; quilted with designs of feathers, scallops, vines & leaves, flowers, butterflies & bows; polyester batting. $535.00

7100990 – JACOB'S LADDER/STREAK OF LIGHTNING; 83" x 93"; colonial blue, turkey red & tan; 100% cotton; made in New York in 1990; machine pieced, free-motion machine quilted; Fairfield Low-Loft Polyester batting, coordinating back. $403.00

7100990

1110990

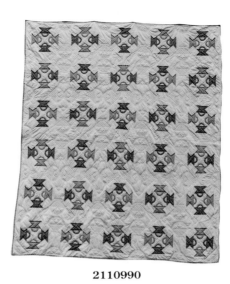

2110990

3110990

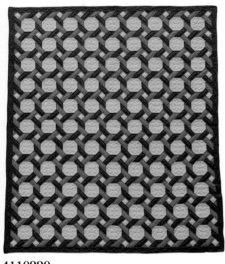

4110990

5110990

6110990

7110990

1110990 – POSTAGE STAMP; 75" x 95"; variegated solids; polyester knits; made in Kentucky in 1989; hand pieced & tied; whip stitch hem around each block, polyester batting, light beige lining, reversible. $173.00

2110990 – POSTAGE STAMP BASKET; 84" x 100"; mauve & seafoam green on off-white background; 100% cotton top & lining; made in Alabama in 1988; hand pieced & quilted; polyester batting. $690.00

3110990 – BURGOYNE SURROUNDED; 68" x 89"; deep wedgwood blue & off-white background; 100% cotton; made in California in 1990; machine pieced, hand quilted; polyester batting, reproduction of an antique quilt, French bias binding. $920.00

4110990 – ROUND THE TWIST; 82" x 98"; burgundy, teal & off-white; 100% cotton; made in Wisconsin in 1984; machine pieced, hand quilted; burgundy has small teal flower & teal has small burgundy flower, quilted around each piece & border, backing is off-white, Mountain Mist batting. $460.00

5110990 – FLOWER GARDEN; 80" x 90"; assorted colors with green & off-white; cotton; made in Illinois in 1990; machine pieced, hand quilted; polyester batting, variety of colors for flowers set together with a diamond of green & off-white. $288.00

6110990 – TRIP AROUND THE WORLD; 84" x 90"; greens, rose & off-white; cotton blends; made in Pennsylvania in 1986; machine pieced, hand quilted; Polyfill Bonded batting. $288.00

7110990 – LAZY DAISY; 78" x 93"; off-white, colonial pink & beige floral; 100% cotton surface, 50/50 backing; made in New York in 1990; machine pieced & quilted; Mountain Mist Poly batting, 30 muslin blocks set together with 20 lazy daisy stars surrounded by pink border embellished with quilted fleur-de-lis design, muslin blocks are quilted with circular floral type design. $575.00

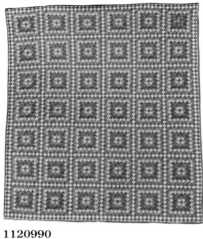

1120990

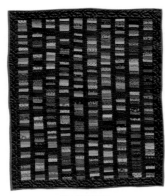

2120990

3120990

4120990

5120990

6120990

1120990 – SMALL BLOCKS; 46" x 81"; jade solid with green prints; all cotton; made in Missouri in 1984; hand pieced & quilted. $328.00

2120990 – FABRIHOLIC'S FANTASY; 29" x 36"; multi-colored with gray & red binding; cotton & cotton blends; made in North Dakota in 1989; hand pieced, machine quilted; made of mail order swatches, signed & dated. $60.00

3120990 – TRIP AROUND THE WORLD; 98" x 98"; mauve & blue print; cotton & cotton blends; made in 1989; machine pieced, hand quilted; off-white muslin lining, has two matching pillow shams. $345.00

4120990 – FLORAL MEDALLION; 74" x 86"; reds, pinks, yellows, blues & greens on white background; cotton; made in Nebraska in 1930's; hand appliqued, quilted & embroidered; cotton batting, scalloped edges, embroidered details on flowers. $1,380.00

5120990 – CROWN OF THORNS; 81" x 96"; brights on black; 100% cotton; made in 1988; machine pieced, hand quilted; 100% pre-washed cotton Amish colors on black, both sides seamed, Mountain Mist Bonded batting. $518.00

6120990 – BUTTERFLIES; 42" x 42"; dusty rose, blue & white; cotton percale; made in South Dakota in 1989; machine appliqued & quilted; crib quilt or wallhanging; Dacron batting. $92.00

7120990 – STRING STAR; 66" x 82"; multi-colors on pink; cotton & cotton blends; top made in Arkansas in 1942, newly quilted; hand pieced & quilted; double bias binding, couple of minor stains. $230.00

7120990

52

1130990

2130990

3130990

4130990

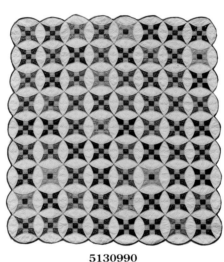

5130990

6130990

7130990

1130990 – PATCHWORK; 80" x 98"; dark blue, dark yellow print; cotton & cotton poly; made in New Mexico in 1980; hand pieced & quilted. $443.00

2130990 – UNTITLED; 90" x 125"; unbleached muslin with blue back; cotton, polyester-cotton; made in Illinois in 1989; hand quilted; unbleached muslin one one side, solid blue on the other. $230.00

3130990 – APPLIQUED ANIMAL DESIGN; 40" x 52"; blue, maroon & tan with background of individual blocks in assorted blended colors; cotton-polyester; made in Arkansas in 1990; hand appliqued & quilted; finished with double binding, polyester batting, 100% washable. $55.00

4130990 – HEART APPLIQUE; 61" x 70"; blue, navy, mauve & burgundy; 100% cotton; made in Kentucky in 1989; machine pieced, hand appliqued & quilted; 100% polyester Poly-fil traditional batting, twenty 6" hearts appliqued on muslin surrounded by 4 borders (2 print & 2 muslin), heart quilting in outer border. $230.00

5130990 – NINE PATCH DINNER PLATE; 78" x 88"; solid gold & brown with brown prints & muslin; poly cotton blends; made in Arkansas in 1990; hand pieced & quilted; Fairfield Traditional batting, quilted with brown thread. $317.00

6130990 – TRIP AROUND THE WORLD; 69" x 87"; pink & blue; cotton; made in New Mexico in 1989; machine pieced, quilted & tied; Mountain Mist batting. $345.00

7130990 – SMALL 8 PT. STAR; 63½" x 86"; tiny mauve rose print with muslin background; 100% cotton; made in Tennessee in 1989; hand pieced & quilted. $345.00

1140990

2140990

3140990

4140990

5140990

6140990

1140990 – IRISH CHAIN; 77" x 96"; red & gold with off-white background; cotton; made in Kentucky in 1989; machine pieced, hand quilted; quilted by the piece, polyester batting, lightweight. $345.00

2140990 – FIELD OF DIAMONDS; 76" x 100"; multi-colors; cotton; made in Washington in 1983; hand pieced & quilted; framed in small black diamonds, light green back, pre-washed fabrics, Mountain Mist batting. $805.00

3140990 – SINGLE IRISH CHAIN; 85" x 95"; black, brown, red & cream on front, brown leaf print & cream on back; 100% cotton, binding is polyester/cotton; made in Vermont in 1990; machine pieced, tied; used Eleanor Burns Quilt In A Day Method. $288.00

4140990 – HOLE IN THE BARN DOOR; 66" x 80"; green, off-white & red; cotton; made c. 1900; hand pieced & quilted; cotton batting, some of old fabrics have faded, excellent condition considering age. $518.00

5140990 – ATTIC WINDOW; 90" x 100"; multi-colors on blue background; cotton & cotton blends; made in Texas in 1987; machine pieced, hand quilted; Hi-Loft batting, quilted in the seams, erasable pen outlining quilting design needs washing out. $403.00

6140990 – FLOWERS; 46" x 51"; pastel greens, pink, purple & mauve; cotton & cotton blend; made in Wisconsin in 1989; machine pieced, hand & machine quilted, hand appliqued & embroidered; poly batting. $87.00

7140990 – ORIGINAL; 39" x 39"; pinks, aquas, black & white; cotton; made in Massachusetts in 1987; machine pieced, hand quilted; cotton batting & back, sleeve for hanging, strip-piecing used, signed & dated. $575.00

7140990

1150990

2150990

3150990

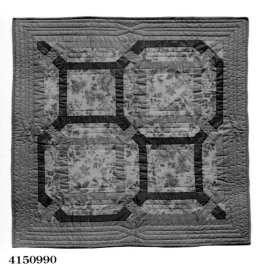

4150990

5150990

6150990

7150990

1150990 – STARS OVER THE MOUNTAIN; 36" x 36"; dusty rose, colonial blue, white & pink; cotton; made in Minnesota in 1990; machine pieced, hand quilted; poly batting. $195.00

2150990 – KANSAS STAR WALLHANGING; 35" x 35"; grayish-grape, raspberry & cinnamon with light mauve background; 100% cotton; made in Indiana in 1989; machine pieced, hand quilted; polyester batting. $110.00

3150990 – LEI KUKUI; 29½" x 29½"; Williamsburg blue applique & border, sky blue background, calico for backing; Imperial Broadcloth, 50/50 cotton/polyester; made in Marshall Islands in 1990; hand appliqued & quilted; Mountain Mist Polyester batting; echo quilting ½" away from one another, washable & dryable, design hand quilted in border. $213.00

4150990 – GARDEN MAZE; 34" x 34"; pink & greens with peach & grays in floral background; polished cotton & cotton; made in Florida in 1986; machine pieced, hand quilted; tube at top for hanging, green bias binding applied with mitered corners, thin polyester batting. $173.00

5150990 – LOG CABIN; 31" x 31"; tones of brown with rust; cotton/poly; made in Illinois in 1989; machine pieced, hand quilted; poly batting. $65.00

6150990 – FUCHSIAS ON BRICK WALL; 29" x 39"; Amish colors; cotton; made in Washington; machine pieced, quilted & appliqued. $156.00

7150990 – DOUBLE IRISH CHAIN; 44" x 48"; pink & dark lavender with white background & eyelet lace; 100% cotton; made in Maryland in 1988; machine pieced, hand quilted; appliqued corner squares, 100% polyester batting. $173.00

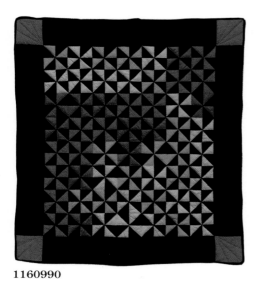

1160990

2160990

3160990

4160990

5160990

6160990

1160990 – 448 TRIANGLES; 55" x 59"; light pinks, peach to hot pink, purple & black, backing is bright pink; 100% cotton; made in California in 1990; machine pieced, hand quilted; poly batting; quilted around each triangle & border, signed & dated. $288.00

2160990 – CHRISTMAS ANIMALS; 44" x 58"; white, red, green & blue; cotton & blends; made in North Carolina in 1980; machine pieced & appliqued, hand quilted; 6 appliqued Christmas animals, matching print background has animals & holly, polyester batting. $98.00

3160990 – SWINGING CORNERS; 24" x 24"; peach, blue & coral; 100% cottons; made in Colorado in 1989; machine pieced, hand quilted; pre-washed, poly batting, curves in this wallhanging give it motion & lots of quilting gives it softness & texture. $87.00

4160990 – CHRISTMAS TREE WALL QUILT; 39" x 39"; red, green & white; 100% cotton Christmas prints; made in Illinois in 1990; machine pieced, hand quilted; unique arrangement of squares & triangles create this "tree within a tree" Christmas wall quilt. $98.00

5160990 – BILLIE BOY; 42" x 52"; blue check with white, shirts multi-colored checks; cotton/poly; made in Illinois in 1989; hand appliqued & quilted; poly batting. $87.00

6160990 – SUMMERHOUSE; 37" x 37"; shades of lavender, green, peach on pale green back with dark purple border; cotton/poly; made in Washington in 1989; hand pieced & quilted; poly batting. $115.00

7160990 – ALPHABET BABY QUILT; 39" x 46"; pastels; cotton/poly; made in Missouri in 1990; machine pieced, hand tied; pastel ginghams & solid with a letter of the alphabet embroidered in each solid block. $60.00

7160990

1170990

2170990

3170990

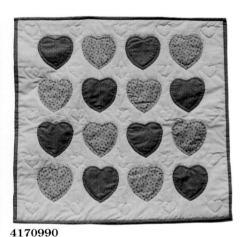

4170990

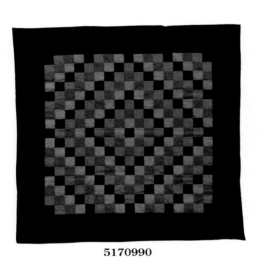

5170990

6170990

7170990

1170990 – ALL WHITE QUILTED; 33" x 45"; all white; broadcloth; made in Arkansas in 1990; hand quilted; the word "Baby" is quilted in center; Mountain Mist polyester batting, border finished with white eyelet ruffle, 100% washable. $55.00

2170990 – EMBROIDERED PATTERN; 76" x 78"; off-white; cotton; made in Ohio circa 1920-1930; cross-stitched, hand quilted; flannel batting; few small age spots. $196.00

3170990 – 8 POINTED STAR; 40" x 40"; red, green & white; polyester/cotton blend; made in Kentucky in 1990; machine pieced, hand quilted; polyester batting, made from Christmas prints with borders added to frame design. $189.00

4170990 – HEARTS; 26½" x 26"; tan & dusty blue print hearts on unbleached muslin background; cotton-cotton blends; made in Nebraska in 1989; hand appliqued & quilted; Polyfil batting, hearts appliqued on background, hanging sleeve on back. $70.00

5170990 – SUNSHINE AND SHADOW; 33" x 33"; black, pink, purple & blue; 100% cotton; made in Pennsylvania in 1989; machine pieced, hand quilted. $115.00

6170990 – NIGHT WINDOWS; 44" x 44"; navy, rust & peach; 100% cotton; made in North Dakota in 1989; hand & machine pieced, hand quilted; sampler of stars ranging from 3" to 6", set in Attic Window blocks, signed & dated. $345.00

7170990 – FAT CHANCE; 47" x 64"; multi-colors with brown border; mostly cotton, few poly-cotton; made in Illinois in 1989; hand & machine pieced, machine quilted; interlocking pattern using free association of prints from the 40's to the 80's, four cut corners give octagonal shape, signed & dated. $184.00

1180990

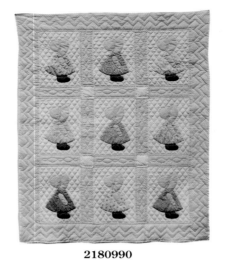

2180990

3180990

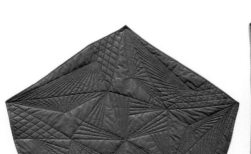

4180990

5180990

6180990

1180990 – LONE STAR; 36" x 36"; red & green on off-white background; cotton, cotton & polyester; made in Minnesota in 1989; machine pieced, hand quilted; Lone Star pattern in Christmas colors, polyester batting, sleeve for hanging on back. $127.00

2180990 – SUNBONNET SUE; 42" x 52"; delicate pink, white & calico; cotton/poly; made in Illinois in 1990; pink check border, pink bonnets & calico dresses (assorted colors), Dacron batting. $87.00

3180990 – UNTITLED; 34" x 34"; muted blue & pink with navy; all cotton, binding is 50% cotton & 50% polyester; made in California in 1986; machine pieced, hand quilted; outline quilted & quilted with star which radiates to four corners, cotton batting, no fading, signed & dated. $92.00

4180990 – MANDALA; 37" from point to opposite side; blue on blue; 100% polished cotton; made in California in 1982; hand quilted. $219.00

5180990 – SPRING STAR; 52" x 52"; peach & green; 100% cotton designer fabrics; made in Ohio in 1989; machine pieced, hand quilted; polyester batting, 100% cotton backing, double fabric binding. $230.00

6180990 – COUNTRY HOME SAMPLER; 32" x 32"; red, green & tan on medium blue background; 50/50 cotton; made in Arkansas in 1990; machine pieced, hand appliqued & quilted; Traditional batting, hearts & little houses quilted around border of applique house; white backing of 50/50 with casings top & bottom for dowels & at top hanging rings. $144.00

7180990 – IRISH CHAIN; 81" x 98"; red check print with off-white muslin background; cotton; made in Kentucky in 1989; machine pieced, hand quilted; polyester batting; quilted by the piece, has hearts quilted on 2 borders & on plain larger blocks. $317.00

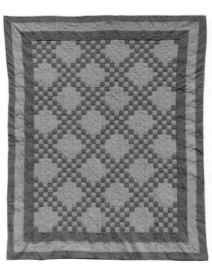

7180990

1190990

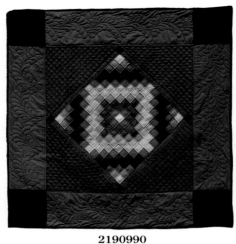

2190990

3190990

4190990

5190990

6190990

7190990

1190990 – BASKET OF FLOWERS; 91" x 95"; blue, cranberry & rose; all 100% cotton; made in Tennessee in 1989; hand quilted & appliqued; 30's look with natural muslin background, blue checkered baskets with matching solid blue bows. $575.00

2190990 – AMISH DIAMOND; 50" x 50"; black, dark red, shades of greens, blues & lavenders; broadcloth; made in Pennsylvania in 1990; machine pieced, hand quilted; 100% polyester batting, washable, each block quilted, a feather design in border. $345.00

3190990 – STRIP PIECING; 38" x 38"; multi-colored with black; cotton, cotton blends; made in Texas in 1990; machine pieced, hand quilted; poly batting. $115.00

4190990 – FARM ANIMALS; 33" x 44"; brown & off-white; cotton/poly; made in Illinois in 1989; pre-printed blocks, machine pieced, hand quilted; poly batting. $70.00

5190990 – MAPLE LEAF; 78½" x 98½"; multi-colored leaves, green set in strips; leaves are cotton, polyester, blocks are unbleached muslin; made in New York in 1979; hand pieced, appliqued & quilted; sheet backing, traditional polyester batting. $345.00

6190990 – FLOWER PATCH; 84" x 98"; white, greens, orange, yellow, pink & blue with pink binding; made in 1986; hand quilted & appliqued; Mountain Mist Poly batting. $575.00

7190990 – TRIP AROUND THE WORLD; 75½" x 95½"; rose, dusty green, deep green on rose background; 100% cotton front & broadcloth backing; made in Michigan in 1990; machine pieced, hand quilted; quilted in floral motif & diamond pattern through matching colors, Cotton Classic batting. $345.00

1011290

2011290

3011290

4011290

5011290

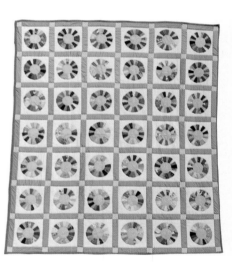

6011290

7011290

1011290 – BIRDS IN FLIGHT; 78" x 90"; variegated print blocks with muslin background; cotton & blends; made in Arkansas in 1988; hand & machine pieced; off-white muslin backing, Lo-Loft polyester batting. $230.00

2011290 – TRIANGLE TWIST; 90" x 108"; mauve & blue with dark blue backing; 100% cotton; made in Alabama in 1990; machine pieced, hand quilted; Hobbs polyester batting. $575.00

3011290 – TUMBLER; 80" x 92"; multicolored; cotton; made in Washington; machine pieced & quilted; Charm quilt with 500 different fabrics in tumbler pattern, Extra Loft Poly batting. $863.00

4011290 – AUTUMN STAR; 97" x 116"; antique gold, brown rust, turquoise, aqua; cotton, cotton/polyester; made in Illinois in 1988; machine pieced, hand & machine quilted; Bonded polyester batting, reversible with complementary polyester/cotton fabric, signed & dated. $460.00

5011290 – DOUBLE WEDDING RING; 87" x 102"; multicolors with white background; cotton; made in 1940's; machine pieced, hand quilted; cotton batting, very soft feel, crosshatch & floral pattern stitches, 2 worn spots on 2 small squares. $265.00

6011290 – LOVE RINGS; 74" x 86"; light green & yellow with multicolored fabrics in circles; cotton; made in Arkansas in 1989; hand appliqued, machine pieced blocks & sashes, hand quilted; Mountain Mist batting, fabrics reminiscent of the 30's, pre-washed, back is unbleached cotton. $259.00

7011290 – PONTOROSA ROSE; 90" x 104"; off-white; made in Tennessee in 1990; hand pieced & quilted. $575.00

1021290

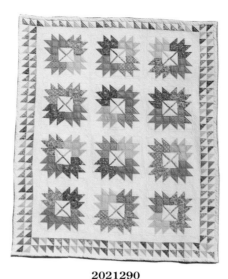

2021290

3021290

4021290

5021290

6021290

1021290 – IRISH CHAIN; 86" x 102"; black with red & blue; broadcloth; made in Pennsylvania in 1989; machine sewn, hand quilted; poly batting, 100% washable, lots of quilting. $575.00

2021290 – MAPLE LEAF; 78" x 95"; green & fall colored leaves on cream background; unbleached muslin lining & background with polyester/cotton blend leaves; made in Idaho in 1990; machine pieced & hand quilted; polyfil batting, queen size coverlet. $460.00

3021290 – WEDDING RING; 93" x 93"; white, gold & yellow; poly cotton broadcloth; made in Missouri in 1990; machine pieced & hand quilted; polyester bonded batting, signed & dated. $345.00

4021290 – UNKNOWN; 88" x 102"; blue star on white; 100% cotton; made in Iowa in 1989; top is machine sewn, rest is hand quilted; Mountain Mist batting. $345.00

5021290 – BRICKWALK; 84" x 107"; multicolor scrap, red/lavender/navy blue border with light blue print backing; 100% cottons; made in Pennsylvania in 1990; machine pieced, hand quilted; 100% traditional polyester batting, quilted ¼" inside each brick, lavender in border is 3-D, rod pocket for hanging, double bias binding, signed & documented. $748.00

6021290 – QUEEN ANNE'S PETTICOAT; 78" x 101"; dark country blue, off-white, gray paisley with emerald green accent; cotton, cotton/poly blends; made in Minnesota in 1982; machine pieced, hand quilted; Mountain Mist polyester batting, signed. $288.00

7021290 – CORNERSTONE LOG CABIN; 81" x 98"; mauve, rose & pink; cotton-polyester blend; made in Missouri in 1990; machine pieced, hand quilted; polyester batting, variation of Log Cabin with small squares called Cornerstones, logs are 1½" wide. $403.00

7021290

1031290

2031290

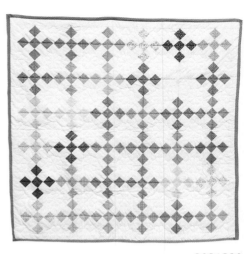

3031290

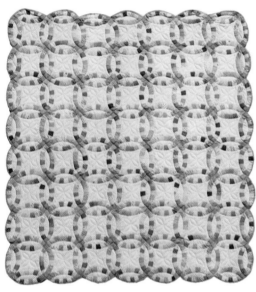

4031290

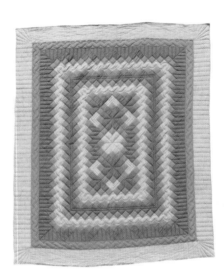

5031290

6031290

7031290

1031290 – RAIL FENCE; 92" x 110"; red, yellow & blue print with blue back; cotton polyester; made in Illinois; hand quilted; country look, fresh bright colors. $190.00

2031290 – TRIP AROUND THE WORLD; 74" x 97"; shades of green; 100% cotton; made in Vermont in 1990; machine pieced & tied; bonded polyester batting, carefully sewn using Eleanor Burns Quilt-In-A-Day method. $259.00

3031290 – NINE PATCH SCRAP QUILT; 52½" x 54½"; scrap quilt of pastel prints, set in muslin; 100% cotton; made in Connecticut in 1990; hand quilted; polyester batting, 6" 9-patch blocks in pastel prints set diagonally with plain muslin blocks, country blue bias binding. $230.00

4031290 – DOUBLE WEDDING RING; 94" x 107"; country blues, mauves & greens with cream background & mauve print lining; cotton/poly; made in Missouri in 1990; machine pieced, hand quilted; poly batting. $403.00

5031290 – BLUE SKIES; 86" x 107"; blue & white; cotton blends & cotton; made in Pennsylvania in 1990; machine pieced, hand quilted; bonded polyester fiber. $403.00

6031290 – SAMPLER; 72" x 84"; assorted colors, gold sashing, pink & blue borders; cotton & poly cotton; made in Louisiana in 1989; hand & machine pieced, hand quilted; polyester batting, poly cotton backing, made by African-American quilter listed on register of Louisiana folk craftspeople. $173.00

7031290 – STAR MEDALLION; 85½" x 85½"; pink & black/tan/pink print; 100% cotton; made in New York in 1989; machine pieced, hand quilted; quilted in off-white & black thread, double binding, pre-washed, thin poly batting, signed & dated. $460.00

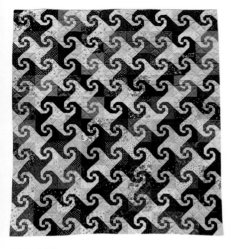

1041290

2041290

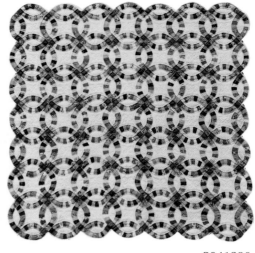

3041290

4041290

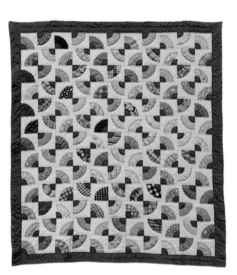

5041290

6041290

1041290 – SNAILS TRAILS; 91" x 102"; light & dark prints; cotton-poly mix; made in Oregon in 1990; machine pieced, hand quilted; double bias binding, Dacron batting. $345.00

2041290 – BRIDAL WREATH; 86" x 104"; slate blue & rose; cotton; made in Kansas in 1990; hand quilted & appliqued; poly filled batting, mitered corners, double binding, signed & dated. $489.00

3041290 – WEDDING RING; 96" x 96"; beige, brown, mauve, blue, stripe, various shades of each; polyester & cotton; made in Illinois in 1989; machine pieced, hand quilted; Hobbs batting, numerous colors that coordinate set together with off-white, backing is off-white. $397.00

4041290 – BUSY BUTTERFLIES; 85" x 95"; pinks, multicolors, background is off-white & pale pink; poly cotton; made in Indiana in 1989; machine pieced & appliqued, hand quilted; poly-cotton batting. $748.00

5041290 – FAN; 83" x 85"; mixed prints, blue border with off-white background; cotton; quilted in Tennessee in 1989; hand pieced & quilted; polyester batting, older 30's top that has been newly quilted, lots of different 30's prints. $403.00

6041290 – OCEAN WAVES; 78" x 88"; multi-color waves, white backing, binding & background; cotton; made in South Dakota in 1988; hand pieced & quilted; regular Mountain Mist batting, very colorful. $374.00

7041290 – MORNING STAR; 80" x 96"; blue, peach & off-white; cotton & polyester; made in Illinois in 1990; machine pieced, hand quilted; Dacron batting, off-white cotton & polyester backing. $460.00

7041290

63

1051290

2051290

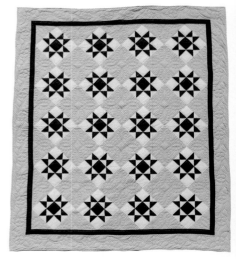

3051290

4051290

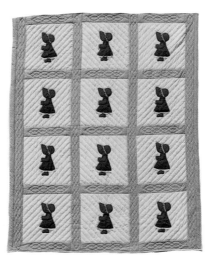

5051290

6051290

7051290

1051290 – MARBLE FLOOR; 78" x 90"; browns, pinks, blues, off-white prints, back is white on beige print; cotton designer fabrics, poly-cotton, cotton broadcloth; made in Colorado in 1990; machine pieced & quilted; Mountain Mist polyester batting, fabrics have a watercolor effect which makes you think of marble tiles, piecing pattern & contrasting quilting pattern help blend fabrics into tiles, quilt is soothing but not boring to view. $380.00

2051290 – BURSTING STAR; 90" x 108"; off-white floral background, blue floral, cranberry, rose; 100% cotton; made in New York in 1990; machine pieced, free-motion machine quilted; double hand sewn binding, Fairfield "Low-Loft" polyester batting. $403.00

3051290 – OHIO STAR; 82" x 97"; pink, green with ecru background; 100% cotton; made in Pennsylvania in 1990; machine pieced, hand quilted; Fairfield 100% bonded polyester batting, unbleached muslin backing, feathers quilted on alternate pink blocks, Ohio Stars outline quilted, border has flowers quilted on vine. $633.00

4051290 – SPRING STAR; 91" x 97"; star & flowers in shades of purple & lavender with white background; cotton-polyester blend; made in Missouri in 1990; machine pieced, hand quilted; Hi-loft polyester batting, star in center with tulip blocks to fill in around the star, diamond-pieced border in 2 colors of lavender, borders are hand quilted in tulip pattern. $403.00

5051290 – SUE; 79" x 102"; blue print & solid with white lace on cream background; cotton/polyester; made in Missouri in 1990; machine pieced & appliqued, hand quilted; poly batting. $345.00

6051290 – IRISH CHAIN; 83½" x 100"; mauve/cream; 100% cotton; made in Tennessee in 1990; machine pieced, hand quilted; polyester batting, lightweight with tiny mauve roses print, has quilted rope-like border, 1 minor stain. $374.00

7051290 – LOG CABIN FAN; 80" x 102"; shades of rose, beige & white; all cotton with poly cotton back; made in Kansas in 1989; machine pieced, hand quilted; poly filled batting, mitered corners, double binding, bows quilted in corner of fans, signed & dated. $460.00

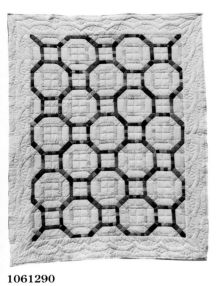

1061290

2061290

3061290

4061290

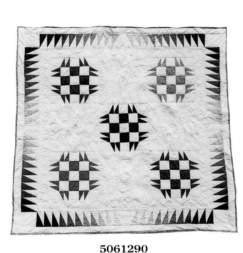

5061290

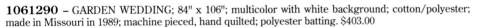

6061290

1061290 – GARDEN WEDDING; 84" x 106"; multicolor with white background; cotton/polyester; made in Missouri in 1989; machine pieced, hand quilted; polyester batting. $403.00

2061290 – LEAVES; 72" x 84"; multicolored leaves with yellow sashing & white background; cotton, cotton blends; made in North Carolina in 1980; machine pieced, hand appliqued & quilted; poly batting. $345.00

3061290 – TENNESSEE WALTZ; 72" x 89"; deep rose, pink & off-white with off-white backing; 100% cotton; made in California in 1987; machine pieced, hand quilted in the ditch on pieced blocks; polyester batting, feathered wreath in plain blocks. $403.00

4061290 – TRIP AROUND THE WORLD; 80" x 94"; variegated prints & solids; soft polyester knits; made in Kentucky in 1986; hand pieced, machine quilted with loop design; polyester batting, blue lining. $202.00

5061290 – PIGEON TOES; 88" x 88"; gradated blues with muslin background; cotton, poly/cotton; made in New York in 1990; machine pieced & quilted; poly batting, nine 20" center blocks, 5 pieced & 4 plain muslin, muslin border, then pieced triangles border & another muslin border & bound with blue floral print. $518.00

6061290 – WILD GOOSE; 75" x 103"; brown prints with beige; polyester cotton; made in Nebraska in 1988; hand pieced & quilted; polyester batting. $403.00

7061290 – TESSELATING SQUARES; 79" x 99"; brown solid & brown & off-white print; cottons; made in Kansas in 1980; hand quilted, machine pieced; polyester batting, bold graphic design. $345.00

7061290

1071290

2071290

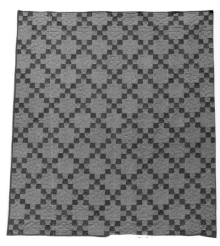

3071290

4071290

5071290

6071290

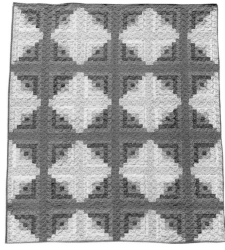

7071290

1071290 – KING'S X; 66" x 102"; light blue, blue print & pink with off-white background, dark blue strips & complementary borders; cotton & blends; made in New York in 1990; machine pieced, center of each square is tied with embroidery floss; polyester batting, 15 squares in alternating pattern. $144.00

2071290 – BROKEN STAR; 78" x 98"; red, off-white, green; cotton & cotton blends; made in New Hampshire in 1987; machine pieced, hand quilted; Mountain Mist light poly batting. $805.00

3071290 – SINGLE IRISH CHAIN; 79" x 91"; assorted 100% cotton red prints with mustard color cotton blend background; made in Massachusetts in 1987; hand pieced & quilted; mustard color backing, handmade bias binding, Mountain Mist poly batting, gold quilting thread, no knots, flower design in solid blocks, overall "grid quilting," pre-washed fabrics, signed & dated. $518.00

4071290 – REVERSE ROMAN SQUARE; 74" x 88"; wine, white, light & dark blue; cotton, cotton polyester blend; made in Nebraska in 1989; machine pieced & quilted; Polyfil batting, quilted in diamond pattern, blue print backing. $173.00

5071290 – WEDDING RING; 78½" x 96"; mauve print on cream & mauve print on sandy peach; 100% cotton; made in Michigan in 1990; machine pieced, hand quilted; unbleached muslin seamless back 100% cotton, 20 stitches per inch on both sides, quilted with cables on lattice, entwined rings on border, outline quilting on blocks, Mountain Mist batting, signed & dated. $794.00

6071290 – DOTTED SIXTEENTH; 48" x 48"; black, white & orange; cotton, linen, cotton blends; made in Massachusetts in 1988; machine pieced, hand quilted; cotton batting, backing is also pieced, each of 25 blocks employs same shapes, though there is a variation of fabric within these shapes & blocks are rotated to add interest & "sound." $575.00

7071290 – LOG CABIN SUNSHINE & SHADE; 81" x 96"; light & dark blue; poly-cotton blends; made in Illinois in 1987; machine pieced & quilted; Hobbs bonded polyester batting, blue lining, binding doubled & double stitched. $173.00

66

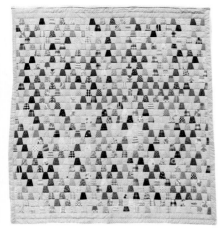

1081290

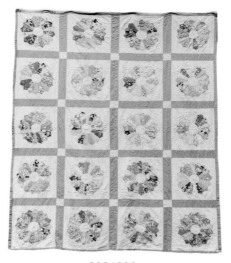

2081290

3081290

4081290

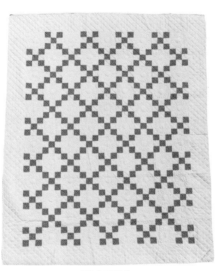

5081290

6081290

7081290

1081290 – TUMBLER; 85" x 95"; variegated prints with yellow; cotton & cotton blends; made in Arkansas in 1990; hand pieced & quilted; muslin backing, muslin double bias binding, polyester batting. $230.00

2081290 – DRESDEN PLATE; 80" x 94"; multicolor with white background & lavender borders; solids & calico cotton; made c. 1940's; machine pieced & appliqued, hand quilted; no batting, backed with floral flannel, few small stains & slight fading. $213.00

3081290 – UNTITLED; 80" x 96"; white, red & green; all cotton; hand appliqued & quilted; very light batting, design in reds is starting to disintegrate but quilting is magnificient, quilted in lines $\frac{1}{16}$" apart, label on back. $547.00

4081290 – FOX AND GEESE; 67" x 81"; predominantly gold & red; cotton; made in Tennessee in 1910; hand pieced & quilted; new border added that a collector could remove if desired, interesting turn-of-the-century prints. $100.00

5081290 – SINGLE IRISH CHAIN or FEATHERED NINE PATCH; 80" x 100"; cream solid & red calico; 100% cottons with muslin back; made in Virginia in 1990; machine pieced, hand quilted; Low loft bonded poly batting, 6" feathered wreaths in plain blocks, heavily quilted, border all cross hatched, double bias binding, signed & dated. $547.00

6081290 – MIDDLE SPREAD OF ROSE SHADING; 86" x 105"; values of blues & roses, off-white & beige; cotton & cotton/poly; made in Ohio in 1990; machine pieced, hand quilted; polyester batting, hand bound with double fabric, original setting with the center spreading out. $472.00

7081290 – FAN; 29" x 35"; multicolor fans on white background with pink & turquoise stripping; cotton; made in Colorado in 1940's; machine pieced, hand quilted; cotton batting, turquoise backing, a doll or baby quilt. $86.00

1091290

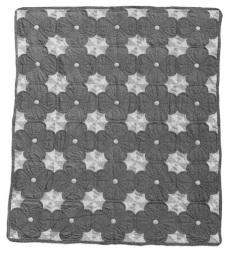

2091290

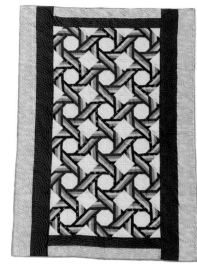

3091290

4091290

5091290

6091290

7091290

1091290 – BUTTERFLY; 78" x 90"; pink & white; cotton; made in Illinois; machine pieced, hand appliqued & quilted; blocks were made by owner's aunt in the 50's & set together by owner in 1974. $173.00

2091290 – BLUE DOGWOOD; 90" x 104"; country blue flowers, yellow centers, leaves are pale green & off-white; poly & cotton broadcloth; made in Kansas in 1990; machine & hand pieced, polyester batting with sheet lining, leaves look like flowers set with spider webs. $345.00

3091290 – AUTUMN WEAVE; 63" x 92"; browns, beige, unbleached muslin & tea dyed muslin; cotton & poly-cotton; made in Indiana in 1990; machine pieced, hand quilted; quilted in-the-ditch on muslin pieces & borders, Mountain Mist batting. $230.00

4091290 – NINE PATCH VARIATION; 65" x 83"; solid peach, white & yellow calico with white background; solids & calico cotton; made c. 1940's; hand pieced & quilted, machine assembled; cotton fabric binding. $202.00

5091290 – RING VARIATION; 75" x 86"; many colors & shades, prints, blue binding, lavender background; cotton; made c. 1940; hand pieced & quilted. $345.00

6091290 – FOUR & NINE PATCH; 70" x 78"; dark shades of wool; made in Missouri in 1990; machine pieced, hand tied with red embroidery floss; red flannel lining & binding, flannel blanket for batting. $202.00

7091290 – OLD FASHIONED ROSE; 73½" x 100"; maroon & green with white background; cotton; made in Texas in 1990; hand appliqued & quilted; cotton batting. $460.00

1101290

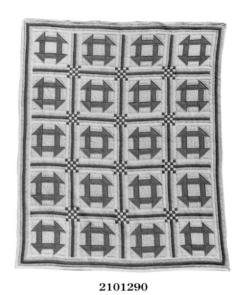

2101290

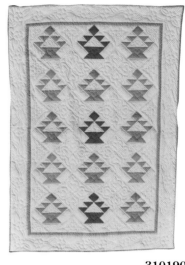

310190

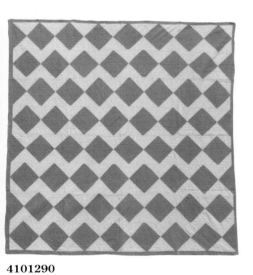

4101290

5101290

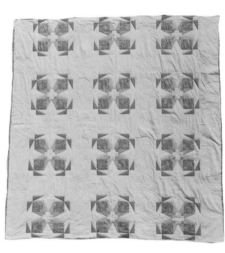

6101290

1101290 – BUTTERCUP; 63" x 95"; gold & white; polyester blends; made in Wisconsin in 1985; hand pieced & quilted; polyester batting, silk-like blended solid gold fabric, also used for backing & edge ruffle. $259.00

2101290 – CHURN DASH; 71" x 86"; purple-violet; cotton & cotton blend; made in Idaho in 1989; machine pieced, hand quilted; Mountain Mist batting. $288.00

3101290 – BASKET; 60" x 93"; pink & rose on white; cotton/poly; made in Illinois in 1989; machine pieced, hand quilted; white backing. $288.00

4101290 – PENNSYLVANIA DUTCH; 80" x 84"; pink & white; made c. 1900?; hand quilted; dark pink print & white with small black print design. $230.00

5101290 – TUNNEL OF LOVE; 76" x 88"; roses, mauves, off-white, blues, tiny bit of green & light brown; cotton & cotton blends; made in Nebraska in 1990; machine pieced, hand quilted; Polyfil batting, quilted in-the-ditch, backing is same mauve print as on front. $282.00

6101290 – ROSE TRELLIS; 52" x 90"; light brown print with peach & teal flower with off-white background; 100% cotton; made in Michigan in 1990; machine pieced, machine & hand quilted; Fairfield bonded polyester batting. $374.00

7101290 – SCOTTIE PUPPIES; 38" x 52"; black, red, white with red & green plaid; cotton & cotton/poly blend; made in Oregon in 1990; machine appliqued, pieced & hand tied; 6 Scottie puppies each have a red bow, red & green tartan plaid borders & back. $50.00

7101290

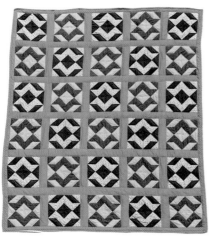

1111290

2111290

3111290

4111290

5111290

6111290

7111290

1111290 – TRIANGLE BUTTERFLY; 78" x 92"; brown, gold & orange; cotton; made in Montana in 1986; machine pieced & quilted; polyester batting, double four patch square of triangles arranged to resemble a butterfly. $518.00

2111290 – DRESDEN PLATE; 80" x 98"; light to dark blue; cotton & polyester; made in Tennessee in 1989; hand pieced & quilted; white backing is 50% cotton & 50% polyester, Mountain Mist 100% polyester batting. $317.00

3111290 – NINE PATCH WITH A FLAIR; 60" x 80"; various prints & solid yellow; cotton & cotton blends; made in Kentucky in 1986; hand pieced, machine quilted; polyester batting. $202.00

4111290 – TRIP AROUND THE WORLD; 65" x 76½"; mixed solids & prints; cotton; made in Kentucky in 1930's; hand pieced & quilted. $213.00

5111290 – BABY QUILT; 38" x 52½"; red & yellow; cotton & cotton flannel; made in California; machine pieced, hand quilted; Fairfield Cotton Classic Batting, quilted with outline & heart-motif quilting pattern, background & backing fabric are pale yellow cotton flannel, signed & dated. $138.00

6111290 – JACOB LADDER VARIATION; 74" x 88"; light purple & white print & cream Jacob Ladder blocks with cream alternating blocks; cotton; machine pieced, hand quilted; light purple binding, white backing, polyester batting, hand quilted ¼" from seam, plain block quilted with 4-petal motif, very faint blue lines where quilted. $460.00

7111290 – HEART QUILT; 40½" x 40½"; blue-green stripe background, hearts are shades of blue; 100% cotton back & top & 100% cotton crochet hearts; made in California in 1990; machine pieced, hand quilted; hand crochet hearts on cotton fabric strips then appliqued onto blocks, polyester batting, 100% cotton white backing, signed & dated. $138.00

1121290

2121290

3121290

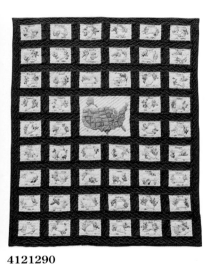

4121290

5121290

6121290

1121290 – TUMBLIN STAR; 92" x 100"; burgundy & rose print stars, green, rose solids, cream & rose print strip; all cotton; made in Alabama in 1987; machine pieced, hand quilted; peach lining, poly batting. $345.00

2121290 – CARPENTER'S WHEEL; 100" x 100"; red & green with natural muslin background; 100% cotton; made in California in 1989; machine pieced, hand quilted; bonded polyester batting. $920.00

3121290 – COUNTRY BRIDE; 90" x 107"; cherry red, country blues, teals, yellow accent tulips with white background; all cotton; made Michigan in 1990; hand appliqued & quilted; signed & dated, seams quilted on both sides, pre-washed fabric, polyester batting, doves over hearts applique, wreaths & hearts quilting. $368.00

4121290 – STATE QUILT; 85" x 105"; multicolor flower & state birds, brown border with white background; cotton & polyester; made in Wisconsin in 1988; hand quilted & embroidered; outline stitch, Fiberfil batting. $2,300.00

5121290 – LOG CABIN; 110" x 110"; brown; cotton; hand pieced & quilted; Mountain Mist batting, pre-washed material. $460.00

6121290 – TRIPLE IRISH HEART; 88" x 110"; white, mauve, light & medium blue; 100% cotton; made in Wisconsin in 1990; machine pieced, hand appliqued & quilted; for a wedding gift, relatives & friends could embroider or write names on hearts. $620.00

7121290 – MARINER STARS; 92" x 111"; blue, green, rose & off-white calicoes; poly-cotton; made in Ohio in 1990, machine pieced, hand quilted, poly-cotton batting. $495.00

7121290

1131290

2131290

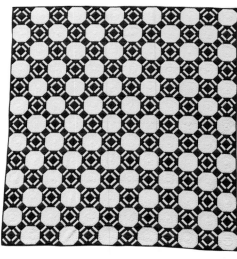

3131290

4131290

5131290

6131290

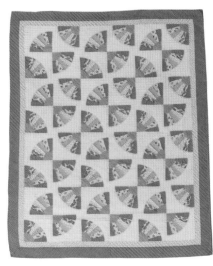

7131290

1131290 – SAMPLER; 74" x 106"; peach, rusts & brown; 100% cotton; made in Idaho in 1989; machine pieced, hand quilted; center motif with sampler blocks, quilted in brown thread, polyester batting, muslin backing. $690.00

2131290 – MONKEY WRENCH; 100" x 100"; teal, dark peacock green & navy print with butterflies; cotton & cotton poly; made in Bermuda in 1989; machine pieced, hand quilted; polyester batting, colors & pattern combine to create an oriental look. $863.00

3131290 – ALABAMA SNOWBALL; 95" x 103"; blue & white; 100% cotton; made in Nevada in 1990; machine pieced, hand quilted; quilted with 78 8" feathered circles, Hobbs batting. $690.00

4131290 – REVERSIBLE QUILT; 44" x 58"; peach floral print; cotton polyester; made in Illinois in 1990; hand quilted; unbleached muslin backing. $50.00

5131290 – SPOOL PATTERN; 86½" x 89"; multicolor spools with white background; cotton & polyester; made in Georgia; machine pieced, hand quilted; light green & kelly green trim. $173.00

6131290 – STARS; 38" x 52"; multicolor on off-white; cotton/poly; made in Illinois in 1989; machine pieced, hand quilted; stars in earth tones & yellow, beige print back. $110.00

7131290 – GRANDMOTHER'S FAN; 84" x 104"; shades of pink on cream background; cotton; made in Kansas in 1990; machine pieced, hand quilted; poly batting, mitered corners, each block trimmed with lace around fan, signed & dated. $483.00

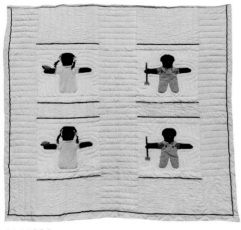

1141290

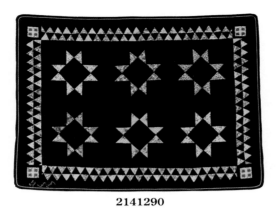

2141290

3141290

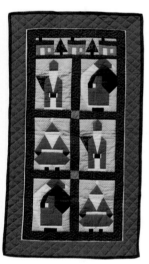

4141290

5141290

6141290

1141290 – DOLL OF THE WORLD; 92" x 96"; lavender & off-white; cottons; made in Louisiana in 1989; hand pieced, appliqued & quilted, embroidered & trapuntoed accents; poly batting, has matching pillow shams, African-American quilter. $685.00

2141290 – PHEBE'S STARS; 44" x 33"; black, yellow, prints; 100% cotton; made in Utah in 1989; machine & hand pieced, hand quilted; binding with piping sewn on by hand, Mountain Mist cotton batting, some 40's & 50's fabrics; signed. $472.00

3141290 – LACE PLAIN; 42" x 54"; beige & white; cotton polyester; made in Illinois in 1990; hand quilted; beige & white strips, some of beige strips are lace, reversible. $55.00

4141290 – SANTAS; 21½" x 41"; tan, forest green, off-white, deep red; cotton; made in Minnesota in 1989; machine pieced, hand quilted; poly batting. $173.00

5141290 – SPLIT RAIL HANGING; 31" x 31"; blue, peach, lilac, mauve; 100% cottons; made in Indiana in 1990; machine pieced, hand quilted; polyester batting, quilted in-the-ditch, Southwest color scheme. $75.00

6141290 – DRESDEN PLATE; 99" x 100"; white background & center with multicolored petals; cotton & polyester; made in Georgia in 1990; machine pieced, hand quilted. $345.00

7141290 – LONE STAR; 66" x 68"; blue, red, orange, dark purple, yellow star with background of white with blue/yellow print flowers; cotton; made in Kentucky c. 1930; hand quilted. $230.00

7141290

73

1151290

2151290

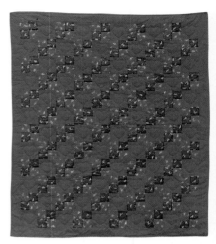

3151290

4151290

5151290

6151290

7151290

1151290 – LOG CABIN STAR; 88" x 102"; shades of blue with white background; all cotton; made in Kansas in 1990; machine pieced, hand quilted; poly batting, mitered corners, signed & dated. $489.00

2151290 – ENCIRCLED TULIP; 86" x 104"; green, rose & white; all cotton with poly cotton backing; made in Kansas in 1990; machine pieced, hand appliqued & quilted; poly batting, double bias binding, signed & dated. $500.00

3151290 – KITTYLAND; 46½" x 54"; red & blue with tiny bits of white & tan; cotton; made in Nebraska in 1989; machine pieced, hand quilted; polyfil batting, alternate blocks of 4 patch & plain blocks, heart is quilted in each plain block, backing is blue kitten print. $155.00

4151290 – PLAIN QUILT; 91" x 115"; peach; unbleached muslin/cotton polyester; made in Illinois in 1990; hand quilted; reversible, light peach on one side, plain unbleached muslin on other. $230.00

5151290 – SAMPLER; 100" x 120"; light gold, rust; cotton & cotton blends; made in Florida in 1985; machine pieced, hand quilted. $195.00

6151290 – JUNGLE LANDING; 40½" x 63½"; reds, greens, blues, brown with pale yellow background & black border; 100% cotton; made in Iowa in 1988; hand pieced & quilted; pre-washed, background is unbleached muslin that is hand-dyed, Low-loft poly batting used with a sheet of Pellon to give stability, stained glass technique used, outline quilting in center, border heavily quilted, signed & dated, sleeve for hanging. $1,150.00

7151290 – ROSE OF SHARON; 47" x 47"; white, pink & green with black border; broadcloth; made in Idaho in 1990; appliqued, hand quilted; Mountain Mist batting, lots of hand quilting. $109.00

1161290

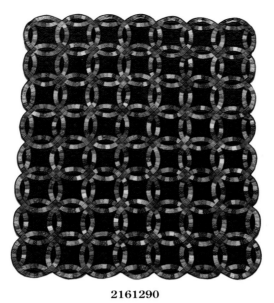

2161290

3161290

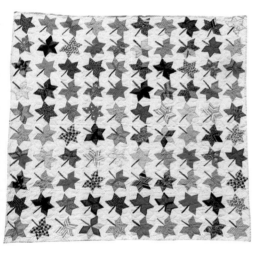

4161290

5161290

6161290

1161290 – DAKOTA SEASONS – WINTER BLIZZARD; 40" x 47"; white on white; cottons, blends, satin, silkies, flannelette & 1 piece velvet, bound in silver lamé; made in North Dakota in 1990; machine pieced & quilted; 9 different pinwheel type blocks in white & off-white fabrics of many textures, lines of trees called shelterbelts in North Dakota are machine embroidered to appear barely discernable as thru a blizzard, quilting lines radiate from house window the way snow looks when falling in front of a light, signed & dated, has rod pocket. $161.00

2161290 – DOUBLE WEDDING RING; 84" x 96"; multicolored on black background; poly/cotton; made in Ohio in 1988; machine pieced, hand quilted; poly batting, old fashioned look. $449.00

3161290 – TULIP GARDEN; 82" x 96"; lavender & pink; pink & rose is cotton blends, rest is cotton; made in Ohio in 1988; hand pieced, quilted & appliqued; polyester filled & backing is cotton blend. $518.00

4161290 – FALLING LEAVES; 84" x 85"; multicolored leaves on white background; cotton & polyester & cotton; made in Kentucky in 1989; machine appliqued & quilted; polyester fiberfill batting, polyester & cotton lining. $173.00

5161290 – PATCHWORK; 74" x 84"; yellow, green, pink, multiple solids & prints; cottons; made c. 1940; hand quilted. $350.00

6161290 – DOGWOOD; 94" x 107"; navy with rose & white corners & padded yellow centers; all cotton; made in Kansas in 1989; machine pieced, hand quilted; has double bias mitered corners, poly backing, poly batting, signed & dated. $489.00

7161290 – PASTEL FOUR PATCH; 34" x 41"; blue, pink & yellow pastels; cotton & poly-cotton blends; made in North Carolina in 1990; machine pieced & quilted; thin polyester batting, muslin backing, neat piecing & diagonal quilting. $98.00

7161290

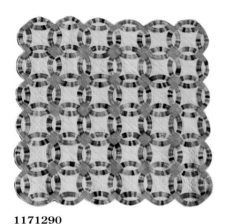

1171290

2171290

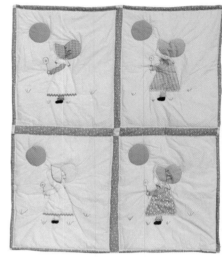

3171290

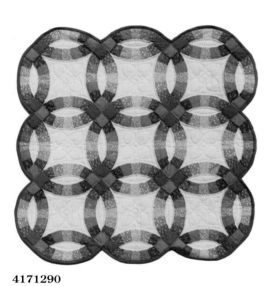

4171290

5171290

6171290

7171290

1171290 – DOUBLE WEDDING RING; 86" x 86"; multicolored on white; cotton & cotton blends; made in 1987; hand pieced & quilted; Mountain Mist batting, older prints. $460.00

2171290 – BLUES MEDLEY; 54" x 66"; blues on white; cotton - cotton/poly; made in Washington in 1990; hand pieced & quilted; fine hand quilting done in pale blue thread. $288.00

3171290 – SUN BONNET GIRLS; 38" x 45"; pinks, purple, greens, reds, white with yellow background; poly cottons & 100% cottons; made in Wisconsin in 1990; hand embroidered, hand & machine appliqued, hand & machine quilted; soft shapes, mixed poly batting. $86.00

4171290 – DOUBLE WEDDING RING; 44" x 44"; dusty blue·with dusty pink flowers; cotton/poly; made in Missouri in 1989; machine pieced, hand quilted; off-white back & background, Dacron batting, Mennonite made, signed & dated. $104.00

5171290 – CARE BEAR; 45" x 56½"; baby yellow, print back, yellow background with pink, blue & gray bears on white clouds; cotton/poly; made in Pennsylvania in 1989; hand quilted; has matching pillow with ruffles, Dacron poly batting. $86.00

6171290 – THE CHRISTIAN SOLDIER; 34" x 36"; soldier on white with royal blue border; poly blend cotton; made in Texas in 1990; hand painted figure, hand quilted, machine sewn; metallic silver fabric paint for shield, helmet & (vest) breast plate, Hobbs poly batting, has rod pocket. $60.00

7171290 – ORIGINAL NATIVE; 62" x 89"; red, green & white; cotton; made in Thailand in 1980; hand made reverse applique. $874.00

1181290

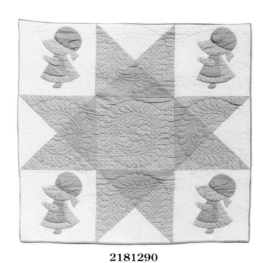

2181290

3181290

4181290

5181290

618190

1181290 – SCRAP BAG STAR; 52" x 52"; brown, beige, bright reds & blues; 100% cotton; made in Maine in 1990; machine pieced, hand quilted; Mountain Mist Quilt Light batting, 100% cotton muslin backing, sleeve for hanging, signed & dated. $196.00

2181290 – SUNBONNET OHIO STAR; 45" x 45"; antique blue & off-white; cotton, cotton & polyester; made in Minnesota in 1989; hand pieced, appliqued & quilted; polyester batting, heavy quilting in feather designs. $196.00

3181290 – FLOWER PATTERN; 43" x 60"; eggshell background with multicolored flowers embroidered around each petal, trimmed with rust material; cotton & polyester, made in Georgia; lined with eggshell eyelet. $60.00

4181290 – IMPROVED FAN; 30" x 30"; multi-colored fabric in fans, off-white background & binding, navy & rust print border; VIP & Concord fabrics; made in Tennessee in 1990; machine pieced, hand quilted. $50.00

5181290 – CUBIC TURTLES; 40" x 55"; purple, turquoise & black with coordinating border print; 100% cotton; made in Illinois in 1990; machine pieced, hand quilted; Mountain Mist 100% Cotton Blue Ribbon batting. $288.00

6181290 – SWALLOWS IN FLIGHT; 48" x 48"; mainly blue with brown swallows, pink flowers & green leaves; 100% cotton front & cotton blend back; made in Washington in 1988; machine pieced, hand quilted; Low-loft batting, hanging sleeve, signed & dated, quilting lines suggest circular pattern of flight. $299.00

7181290 – TEDDY BEAR BABY QUILT; 35" x 40"; pink; 100% cotton; made in Pennsylvania in 1990; mosaic piecing technique. $60.00

7181290

1191290

2191290

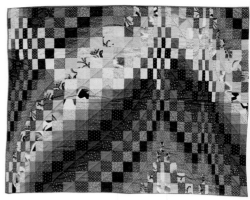

3191290

4191290

5191290

6191290

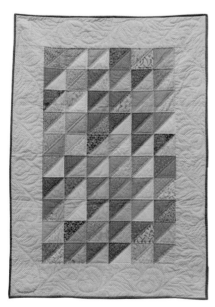

7191290

1191290 – CHAMPAGNE & SHERBET; 33" x 33"; greens; cotton; made in Illinois in 1988; machine pieced & quilted; polyester batting. $92.00

2191290 – COURTHOUSE STEPS; 46" x 56"; black, green, taupe, cream; 100% cotton; made in Wisconsin in 1990; machine pieced, hand & machine quilted; 100% polyester batting, contemporary fabrics & diagonal set give a new look to an old pattern, has hanging sleeve. $345.00

3191290 – SERENDIPITY; 66" x 53"; blue, neutrals, yellow; cotton & blends; made in Pennsylvania in 1989; machine pieced, hand quilted; poly blend batting, signed. $213.00

4191290 – BASKET; 40" x 52½"; white on white & blue green; 100% cottons, pre-washed; made in Colorado in 1990; machine pieced, basket handles hand appliqued, hand quilted; poly batting, heavily hand quilted, signed & dated. $230.00

5191290 – IPU KUKUI (LITTLE LANTERN); 32" x 32"; stream green, teal green; Imperial broadcloth, 50/50 poly/cotton, VIP calico; made in Marshall Islands in 1990; hand appliqued & quilted; Mountain Mist polyester batting, appliqued & quilted in traditional Hawaiian manner with rows of quilting ½" apart. $225.00

6191290 – COLONIAL BLUE SAMPLER; 29" x 29"; colonial blue, rose & ecru; 100% cotton; made in New Hampshire in 1989; machine pieced, hand appliqued & quilted; Low loft batting, pre-washed fabrics. $115.00

7191290 – EVERLASTING SUMMER; 44" x 65"; soft multicolored prints, cream border; 100% cotton; made in Illinois in 1990; hand & machine pieced, hand quilted; 7" wide border, gray & white pin dot binding, light brown paisley backing, polyester batting, signed & dated. $230.00

1010391

2010391

3010391

4010391

5010391

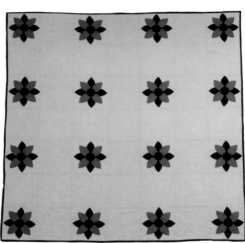

6010391

7010391

1010391 – FLORIDA WINDOW; 37" x 37"; shades of mauve with gray & green flowers on off-white background; polished cotton & cotton; made in Florida in 1986; machine pieced, hand quilted; border quilted in braid, Mountain Mist batting, hanging sleeve, signed & dated. $201.00

2010391 – GRANDMOTHER'S FLOWER GARDEN; 70" x 102"; multicolor flowers bordered in black, unbleached muslin back; cotton & cotton blends; made in Ohio in 1990; hand pieced & quilted; Mountain Mist polyester batting, dated & signed. $230.00

3010391 – STREAK O' LIGHTNING; 60" x 81"; black, brown, green, red, lavender; cotton blends; made in Illinois in 1990; machine pieced & quilted; brown dust ruffle attached for bedspread, cotton polyester batting. $144.00

4010391 – LOG CABIN; 86" x 108"; shades of blue & pink; cotton; made in Kansas in 1990; machine pieced, hand quilted; polyester batting, mitered corners, double binding, signed & dated. $403.00

5010391 – EMBROIDERED; 80" x 80"; off-white with pink sashing; cotton; made in 1930's or 40's; embroidered blocks, machine pieced, hand quilted; some pencil markings of pattern, 8 to 9 st./in., lots of detail. $403.00

6010391 – SPRING GARDEN; 98" x 98"; rust & brown print flowers with beige background; 100% cotton; made in Virginia in 1989; machine pieced, hand appliqued & quilted; polyester traditional batting, lots of quilting, dated. $316.00

7010391 – PEONY; 84" x 100"; rose print, olive green solid on bleached muslin with solid rose back; made in South Carolina in 1990; machine pieced, machine & hand appliqued, hand quilted; double binding, Mountain Mist batting, mitered corners, reversible, outline quilting & varied quilting in solid areas, no seams in lining, rose print flowers with olive green stems & leaves on white background, wine solid borders, signed. $920.00

79

1020391

2020391

302039[

4020391

5020391

602039[

1020391 – SUNFLOWER; 72" x 83"; yellow, orange & tan with brown & green stems, white background; cotton; made in Indiana in 1990; all handmade; polyester batting. $920.00

2020391 – TREE OF LIFE; 87" x 96"; white with blue flowers, some red, orange, yellow; brown & green stems; cotton; made in Indiana in 1989; hand pieced & quilted; polyester batting. $1,725.00

3020391 – CAKESTAND; 38" x 52"; light blues & off-white; cotton, cotton & polyester; made in Minnesota in 1990; hand pieced & quilted; polyester batting, traditional pattern done in soft blues & off-white muslin, hand quilted with heart motifs, hanging sleeve, signed & dated. $190.00

4020391 – CATHEDRAL WINDOW; 100" x 100"; multicolor prints on off-white background; polyester/cotton; made in Tennessee in 1989; machine pieced, hand quilted; polyfil. $1,150.00

5020391 – DUCKY DOODLE; 45" x 60"; yellow duck, orange background, purple borders; cotton; made in Delaware in 1983; hand appliqued, machine pieced, hand embroidery & quilted; polyester batting. $345.00

6020391 – STAR OF SHIRAZ; 34" x 34"; navy, teal, gold with teal & tan background; cotton & cotton/polyester; made in Virginia in 1989; hand pieced & quilted; polyester batting, hexagon shaped, medallion type design, center is 12-point star surrounded by six 8-point stars & print border. $86.00

7020391 – 8 POINT STAR; 94" x 110"; mauve print with navy blue background; poly-cotton blend; made in Missouri in 1987; hand pieced & quilted, seam by seam; polyester bonded batting, royal blue back, reversible. $575.00

702039[

1030391

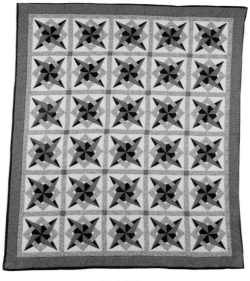

2030391

3030391

4030391

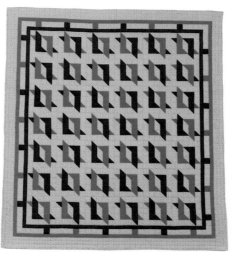

5030391

6030391

7030391

1030391 – TULIPS; 85" x 108"; lavender, blue, ivory background; cotton & cotton blend; made in Nebraska in 1989; hand appliqued, stuffed & quilted, hand marbled fabric; polyfil, appliqued flowers are stuffed so quilt is 3-dimensional. $575.00

2030391 – STARBOUND; 76" x 88"; medium & dark blue with medium pink & muslin; 100% cotton prints; made in Arkansas in 1990; machine pieced, hand quilted; VIP prints, muslin back, Mountain Mist Polyfil batting, bound in dark blue cotton, signed & dated. $345.00

3030391 – FEATHERED STAR; 86" x 94"; tan feathered star with off-white background; made in 1987; machine pieced, hand quilted; Fiber fill fat batting. $431.00

4030391 – CROSS STITCH FLOWER; 71" x 95"; white background with navy & turquoise; cotton & cotton polyester blends; made in Arkansas in 1989; hand embroidered, pieced & quilted; polyester batting, double bias binding. $259.00

5030391 – O.K. SERIES # 1; 76" x 85½"; navy, wine & beige print; cotton; made in New Mexico in 1989; machine pieced & quilted; Mountain Mist batting. $316.00

6030391 – JAPANESE FAN; 104" x 104"; deep country French blues & mauves on pale blue background; cottons & cotton blends; made in California in 1988; machine pieced, hand appliqued & quilted; bonded polyester batting. $690.00

7030391 – APPLIQUED DAISY; 90" x 105"; lavender/white print with yellow center & green leaves; cotton; made in Montana & North Dakota in 1987; hand appliqued, machine pieced & hand quilted; polyester batting, cotton backing, white cotton binding. $403.00

1040391

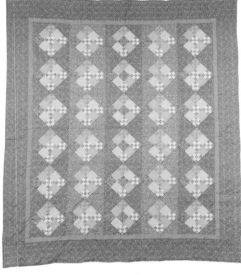

2040391

3040391

4040391

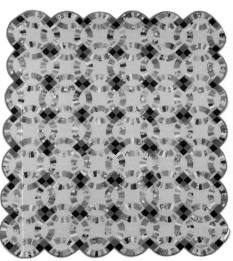

5040391

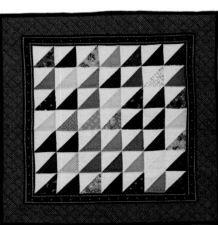

6040391

1040391 – LOVE RING; 92" x 92"; mauve; cotton/polyester; made in Missouri in 1990; machine pieced & quilted; polyester batting. $230.00

2040391 – DOUBLE 9-PATCH; 83" x 96"; pink, blues, white, mauve; all cotton; made in Wisconsin in 1990; machine pieced & quilted, hand bound; Fairfield Co. Batting (poly). $316.00

3040391 – HANGING BASKETS; 17" x 56"; predominantly blue with pink & white accent; cotton & poly/cotton blends; made in Illinois in 1990; hand pieced & quilted; poly batting, mitered stripe border. $65.00

4040391 – CATCHING SOME Z'S; 90" x 96"; navy blue & navy/off-white prints, floral blue print poly cotton backing; cotton top; made in Texas in 1990; machine pieced, hand quilted; Traditional Poly-fil batting, pattern is spin-off of a part of "Around The Twist" pattern, diagonal set with sashing. $391.00

5040391 – DOUBLE WEDDING RING; 82" x 94"; assorted prints with mint green background & lining; cottons & blends; quilted in Virginia in 1985; machine pieced, hand quilted; Polyfil traditional batting, signed & dated. $431.00

6040391 – COUNTRY SCRAPS; 30" x 30"; multicolor triangles paired up with white triangles – all bordered in blue; cotton/poly cotton; made in Pennsylvania in 1990; machine pieced, hand quilted; poly-fil traditional batting. $115.00

7040391 – UNKNOWN; 81" x 93"; blue, yellow, red & green pinwheels with brown print background & red backing; cotton blends; made in Pennsylvania in 1986; machine pieced, hand quilted; Bonded polyester batting. $201.00

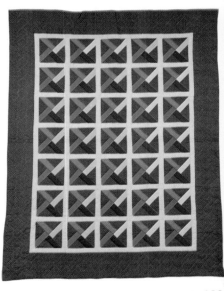

704039

1050391

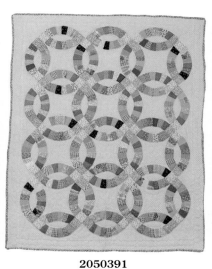

2050391

3050391

4050391

5050391

6050391

7050391

1050391 – RADIANT STAR; 91" x 102"; blue & mauve; cotton-polyester; made in Missouri in 1990; machine pieced, hand quilted; polyester batting. $403.00

2050391 – DOUBLE WEDDING RING; 66" x 82"; multicolor circles with yellow background; cotton; top pieced in 1940's, (quilted in Missouri in 1990); machine & hand quilted; Dacron batting. $138.00

3050391 – LONE STAR; 94" x 100"; blues; cotton-poly; made in Missouri in 1990; machine pieced, hand quilted; polyester batting. $403.00

4050391 – LOG CABIN; 84" x 111"; mauve; cotton-poly; made in Missouri in 1990; machine pieced & quilted; polyester batting. $230.00

5050391 – LARGE BUTTERFLY; 78" x 90"; pink & green; cotton/polyester; made in Missouri in 1990; machine pieced & quilted; polyester batting. $144.00

6050391 – DOUBLE WEDDING RING; 99" x 100"; pale blue, pink & tan, white background & backing; 100% cotton; machine pieced, hand quilted; polyester batting, two inner borders & one outer border with cable quilting pattern, four lobe flowers quilted in white areas, two pillow shams included. $374.00

7050391 – LOVER'S KNOT; 99" x 108"; burgundy, pink & gray, white background & backing; cotton poly blends; made in Illinois in 1990; machine pieced, hand quilted; Dacron batting. $460.00

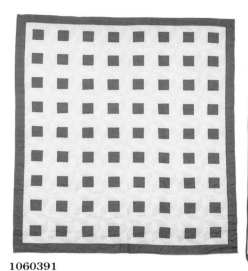

1060391

2060391

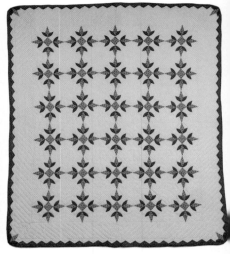

3060391

4060391

5060391

6060391

1060391 – BOX; 80" x 89"; medium blue, pink & white with white broadcloth backing; cotton & cotton blends; made in Arkansas in 1989; machine pieced, hand quilted; blue squares & border have hearts quilted in them, the rest is quilted around each seam, double bias binding, Lo-Loft Polyester batting, non-allergenic. $230.00

2060391 – MILKYWAY; 96" x 100"; peach & green; 100% cotton; made in California in 1990; machine pieced & quilted; 100% polyester batting, allergy free batting. $230.00

3060391 – TURKEY TRACK; 90" x 102"; red print, yellow print on white; cotton; made in California in 1989; hand quilted, hand stitched blocks, straight long border & backing machine stitched; Mountain Mist Dacron polyester batting. $489.00

4060391 – THE HOUSE OF THE WISE; 25" x 33"; black, plum & teal; 100% cotton; made in Texas in 1990; machine pieced, hand quilted; Mountain Mist polyester batting, hanging sleeve, signed & dated. $230.00

5060391 – PRIMROSE PATH; 89" x 102"; values of rose, forest greens, burgundy, solids & prints; 100% cotton; made in Ohio in 1980; hand appliqued & embroidered, machine pieced, hand quilted; polyester batting, double hand bound. $550.00

6060391 – TUNNEL OF LOVE; 85" x 102"; mauve, brown, white with tiny bits of green; cotton, cotton blend; made in Nebraska in 1989; machine pieced & quilted; Polyfil batting. $173.00

7060391 – RAIL FENCE; 72" x 80"; browns (earthtones); 100% cotton; made in Alabama in 1990; machine pieced & quilted, cable borders hand quilted; Hobbs bonded batting, green highlights. $403.00

7060391

1070391

2070391

3070391

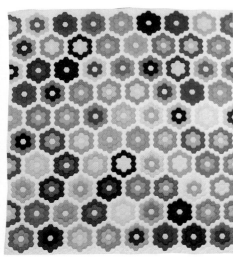

4070391

5070391

6070391

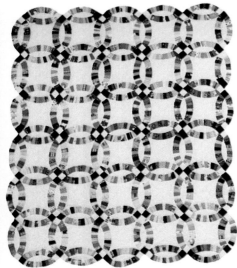

7070391

1070391 – BASKETS; 44" x 46"; pink, blue, yellow, green & lavender print & plain baskets on off-white, dark blue & lavender borders; all cotton; blocks pieced in 1950's, set & quilted in 1990; hand pieced & appliqued on white blocks, blocks & borders machine stitched together, hand quilted; Dacron batting, tiny spot on one block, signed & dated. $144.00

2070391 – CROWN AND THORN; 86" x 102"; pink & green pastels, white; broadcloth & cotton; made in Tennessee in 1990; hand pieced & quilted; polyester batting, bleached sheet lining. $460.00

3070391 – EIGHT POINTED STAR; 90" x 110"; navy, red checked, yellow; cotton & cotton blends; made in Kansas in 1987; machine pieced, hand quilted; old traditional pattern & combination of colors. $345.00

4070391 – GRANDMOTHER'S FLOWER GARDEN; 84" x 92"; multicolor with yellow centers on off-white background; cottons; made in Pennsylvania in 1989; machine pieced, hand quilted; poly batting, quilted in circles around flower. $920.00

5070391 – ROSE APPLIQUE; 75½" x 77½"; roses with green leaves on white background; cotton; made in early 1990's; hand quilted; buttonhole stitch outlining each rose & leaf, two borders were removed due to wear but rest of quilt is in good condition. $207.00

6070391 – FAN; 80" x 94"; fans are shades of blue on white background; cotton; made in Illinois in 1990; machine pieced, hand quilted; polyester batting. $276.00

7070391 – DOUBLE WEDDING RING; 89" x 106"; multicolor rings on white background; cotton/poly; made in Missouri in 1990; machine pieced, hand quilted; Dacron batting, white lining, white double binding, quilted in the ditch around each piece, bells quilted in center. $431.00

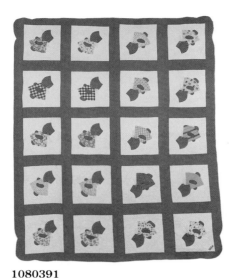

1080391

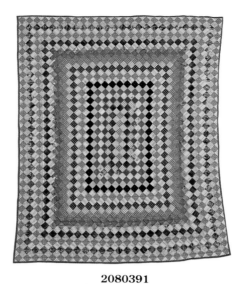

2080391

3080391

4080391

5080391

6080391

1080391 – SUNBONNET BABY; 85" x 68"; multicolor dresses & bonnets on white background set together with blue; all cotton; made in Kansas in 1930; hand embroidered, appliqued, pieced & quilted. $863.00

2080391 – TRIP AROUND THE WORLD; 72" x 85"; variety of colored calico prints, blues predominate, some reds, navy, yellow, green; cottons & blends; made in Virginia in 1990; hand pieced, quilted & bound. $322.00

3080391 – FLORAL BASKET; 80" x 96"; brown basket, green, yellow, blue, 2 shades red & 2 shades peach, white background; cotton; hand embroidered & quilted; 100% polyester batting, includes 25" x 20" pillow sham. $403.00

4080391 – BEAR'S PAW; 84" x 94"; multicolored bear paws with tea-dyed background; 100% cotton; made in Massachusetts in 1990; machine pieced, hand quilted; Fairfield Cotton Classic batting, double thickness binding. $690.00

5080391 – KEEPING THE LIGHT; 41" x 47"; red, white & blue on light gray background, backing is blue with stars; cotton, poly cotton; made in Wisconsin in 1990; hand pieced, appliqued, embroidered & quilted; poly batting. $115.00

6080391 – HOUSES; 70" x 92"; medium blues, off-white muslin, misc. other fabrics; cottons; made in Texas in 1990; hand & machine pieced, embroidery & applique; Fairfield polyfil batting, made as a fund raiser. $575.00

7080391 – FALL QUILT; 56" x 56"; yellow, red, gold, green, rust & brown calicoes, gray pindot squirrels; cotton; made in Pennsylvania in 1989; hand appliqued, machine pieced, hand quilted; Mountain Mist batting. $230.00

7080391

86

1090391

2090391

3090391

4090391

5090391

6090391

7090391

1090391 – NOSEGAY OF FLOWERS; 78" x 89"; pastel fabrics of 1930's, blue-green borders & muslin background & back; made in Michigan; hand quilted; soft pastel fabrics, cotton batting, original quilting between nosegays, 2 different cable designs on the inside border & edge. $374.00

2090391 – SUNRISE; 50" x 33"; blues, greens, grays, yellow with black background & backing; made in Virginia in 1990; machine pieced, hand quilted; poly batting, has hanging sleeve. $201.00

3090391 – NATURAL MOVEMENT; 52" x 35½"; grays, blues, browns, pinks, tans & a dash of purple & green; cottons, poly/cotton; made in Colorado in 1990; machine pieced & quilted; Mountain Mist polyester batting, quilted with silver metallic thread, corded piping sewn into binding. $265.00

4090391 – DOUBLE WEDDING RING; 74" x 96"; pink & green flower print on off-white muslin with pink & dark green polka dot square inserts; 100% cotton; made in Massachusetts in 1987; hand pieced & quilted; Mountain Mist poly batting, flower quilting in centers & overall outline quilting, handmade bias binding, signed & dated. $518.00

5090391 – ROSE WREATH; 82" x 82"; pink, rose, green & yellow on white or cream background; 100% cotton; made in Georgia in 1920; hand appliqued & quilted; cotton batting, border is typical vine array with quilting throughout echoeing applique. $1,380.00

6090391 – ALMOST AMISH; 50" x 63"; green, black, dark solids; cotton & cotton blends; made in Colorado in 1990; machine pieced, hand quilted, Mountain Mist Low Loft batting, black backing, signed & dated. $288.00

7090391 – LITTLE MEDALLION SAMPLER; 32" x 32"; brown, gold, rust, green on cream background, dark brown binding, muslin backing; 100% cotton; made in Illinois in 1985; machine pieced, hand quilted; polyester batting, center 12" block is Gentleman's Fancy, 6" corner blocks are Friendship Star, Double X, Formal Garden, Shoo-fly, has hanging sleeve, signed & dated. $92.00

1100391

2100391

310190

4100391

5100391

6100391

1100391 – LOG CABIN, ARROW PATTERN; 100" x 100"; earth tones; 100% cotton; made in Ohio in 1988; machine pieced, hand quilted; polyester bonded batting, quilt was rinsed to remove all markings. $518.00

2100391 – DAHLIA; 43" x 43"; shades of lavender, ivory & navy; 100% cotton; made in Indiana in 1989; machine pieced, hand quilted; polyester batting, signed & dated. $104.00

3100391 – OKLAHOMA STAR; 25" x 26"; light green, dark green, off-white; cotton; made in North Dakota in 1990; machine pieced & quilted; polyester batting, has rod pocket, signed & dated. $50.00

4100391 – WILD GOOSE TREE; 50" x 50"; forest green with sky blue background, brown tree trunks; made in Tennessee in 1989; hand pieced & quilted; Mountan Mist batting, pieced areas are quilted by the piece & open areas quilted with a dogwood flower, has rod pocket. $316.00

5100391 – FRAGMENTED THOUGHT; 56" x 38"; gray, mauve & cranberry; cotton blends; made in Pennsylvania in 1989; machine pieced, hand quilted; polyester batting. $230.00

6100391 – LOG CABIN; 83" x 84"; rusts, browns, cream & green; cotton & cotton blend; made in Nebraska in 1989; machine pieced & quilted; polyfil batting. $173.00

7100391 – WHIRLIGIG; 72" x 87"; scraps on yellow print background; cottons; made in Kansas c. 1940's; machine pieced, hand quilted; lightweight filler. $299.00

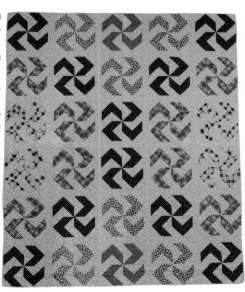

7100391

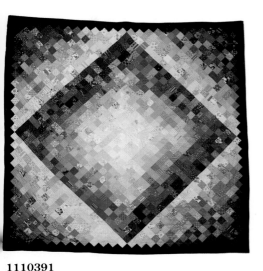

1110391

2110391

3110391

4110391

5110391

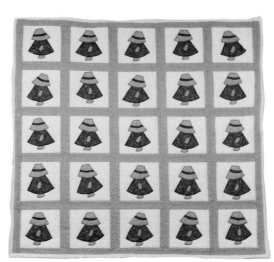

6110391

7110391

1110391 – RADIANCE; 88" x 88"; multicolor with black border; cotton & cotton-polyester blends; made in Arizona in 1989; machine pieced, hand quilted; center is appliqued to border, polyester batting, charm quilt with 1,227 different print & solid fabrics, quilting is an overall starburst pattern. $998.00

2110391 – DOUBLE IRISH CHAIN; 96" x 96"; mint green, mint green calico & white; 50/50 cotton /polyester; made in Illinois in 1989; machine pieced, hand quilted; polyester batting, green back, reversible. $345.00

3110391 – LOG CABIN (Quillow); 41½" x 51½"; blue & white prints, blue back; cotton; made in California in 1990; machine pieced, hand quilted & tied; polyfil batting, folds up into pocket on back & becomes a pillow, great for snuggling, in the grandstand or for traveling. $115.00

4110391 – AROUND THE WORLD; 74" x 94"; multicolored with off-white, purple & pink border; 100% cotton; top made in 1921, quilted in 1988; hand quilted; traditional polyester batting. $316.00

5110391 – UNKNOWN; 80" x 96"; slate blue; cotton & poly; made in Pennsylvania in 1990; hand quilted; Dacron poly batting, reversible. $345.00

6110391 – SUNBONNET SUE; 91½" x 92"; green & rose; cotton; made in Georgia in 1989; hand pieced, quilted & appliqued; polyester fill, white cotton lining. $345.00

7110391 – LITTLE HOUSE; 94" x 94"; multicolor houses with off-white background; cotton-poly mix; made in Oregon in 1990; machine pieced, hand quilted; houses set with chain lattice & off-white background, Dacron batting, light blue backing. $345.00

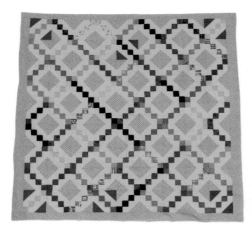

1120391

2120391

3120391

4120391

5120391

6120391

1120391 – JACOB'S LADDER; 69" x 72"; red, blue, white with white background; cotton; made in North Carolina in 1940's; hand pieced & quilted; sheet used for batting, red print in background & border has tiny hearts. $489.00

2120391 – HEARTS AND NINE PATCHES; 38" x 46"; blue print 9-patches, pink hearts on muslin; cottons & blends; made in North Carolina in 1990, machine pieced, appliqued & quilted, muslin backing, polyester batting. $115.00

3120391 – RUBIC'S CUBE STAR; 90" x 108"; 5 shades of blue, green & red on black background; broadcloth; made in Pennsylvania in 1989; machine pieced, hand quilted; polyester batting. $575.00

4120391 – SUNSHINE AND SHADOW; 38½" x 38½"; purples, blues, greens; rayon crepe; made in Pennsylvania; machine pieced, hand quilted. $230.00

5120391 – SUNBURST (Broken Star); 88" x 89"; off-white solid blocks; cotton; made in Missouri prior to 1940; hand pieced & quilted; ornate center then lighter orange, orange-gold, gold, light gold & off-white, heavily quilted ¼" from seams. $920.00

6120391 – EMBROIDERED BUTTERFLIES; 74" x 87½"; light blue sashing with off-white background & multicolored embroidered butterflies; 100% cottons; made in New York in 1989; hand embroidered & quilted; poly batting. $345.00

7120391 – MEXICAN STAR; 61½" x 61½"; blue calico, solid wine, blue/wine print on cream; 100% cotton; made in Kentucky in 1990; machine pieced, hand quilted; polyfil traditional batting, double fold bias binding, 12" Mexican square blocks with 1½" wide lattice strips, quilted border, slate blue backing is 100% cotton, signed & dated. $345.00

7120391

1130391

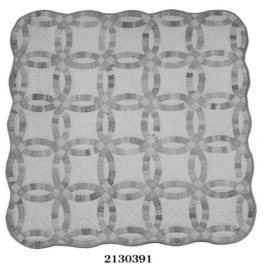

2130391

3130391

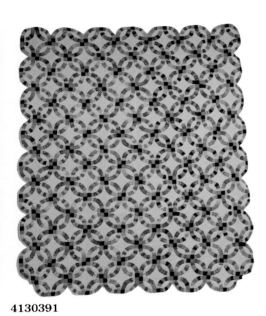

4130391

5130391

6130391

7130391

1130391 – RADIANCE; 27½" x 33"; blues, rose, deep rose, tan; cotton; made in Connecticut in 1987; machine pieced, hand quilted; poly-fil batting, this artistically pieced wallhanging radiates from the center but immediately pulls you back, created with a pleasing blend of blues & roses, this intricately pieced 1½" triangled center & mitered right angles demonstrates a skilled hand that made every point meet. $104.00

2130391 – DOUBLE WEDDING RING; 93" x 93"; light blue & yellow are dominate colors with soft prints; cotton; made in Alabama in 1989; machine pieced, hand quilted; polyester batting. $403.00

3130391 – UNKNOWN; 96" x 105"; navy blue, red, beige, off-white; cotton; made in South Dakota in 1990; machine pieced, hand quilted; "cheater" blocks in between red sashes. $805.00

4130391 – DOUBLE WEDDING RING; 85" x 107"; purple & lavender squares combined with multi-colored prints on off-white background; cotton; made in Illinois in 1990; machine & hand pieced, hand quilting; purple & lavender corners are combined with multicolored prints, a spider web is quilted in each block. $345.00

5130391 – ORIGINAL; 67" x 92"; dark brown & gold with off-white background, animal/bird printed squares; poly-blend cotton; made in Texas in 1990; hand quilted after machine stitched top; Hobbs bonded batting, printed squares of ducks, birds & animals are outlined hand quilted, brown border has hand quilted random leaf border around the quilt. $230.00

6130391 – YELLOW LONE STAR; 88" x 98"; yellow with off-white; 100% cotton; made in Missouri in 1988; polyester & cotton batting. $305.00

7130391 – SAMPLER; 83" x 98"; muslin & assorted solids, back of quilt is muslin; 100% cotton; made in Mississippi in 1990; machine pieced, hand quilted; polyester batting. $345.00

91

1140391

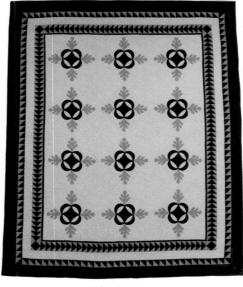

2140391

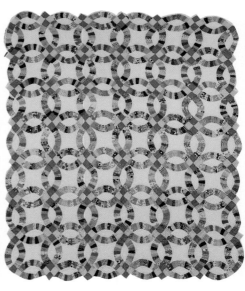

3140391

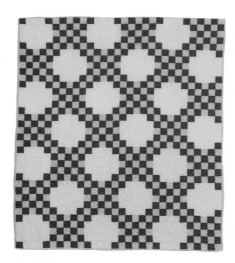

4140391

5140391

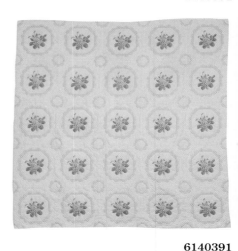

6140391

1140391 – UNKNOWN; 54" x 75"; pink, brown, lavender, off-white, solid white backing; all cotton; made in New York in 1989; hand & machine pieced, hand quilted, poly batting, part of bottom border is not showing in photo. $345.00

2140391 – OAK LEAF; 90" x 110"; cream, navy, burnt peach; 100% cotton, pre-washed; made in Colorado in 1990; hand appliqued, machine pieced, hand quilted; poly batting, Wild Goose Chase & Saw-tooth borders, signed & dated. $748.00

3140391 – DOUBLE WEDDING RING; 78" x 90"; various colors in rings with white background & back; 80% cotton & 20% polyester; made in Iowa in 1985; machine sewn top, hand quilted; 100% polyester batting. $345.00

4140391 – DOUBLE IRISH CHAIN; 77" x 89"; turkey red & off-white; cotton; made in Missouri in 1985; machine pieced; polyfil, center blocks are quilted in hearts & squares. $345.00

5140391 – UNTITLED; 35" x 39"; black, white & red; 100% cotton; made in Wisconsin in 1990; machine pieced, machine & hand quilted; cotton batting, rod pocket on back. $230.00

6140391 – VIOLETS; 79" x 79"; pink, purple & green on white background; cotton; made in Maryland in 1990; machine pieced, hand embroidered, cross stitch & quilted; Mountain Mist polyester batting. $489.00

7140391 – GRANDMOTHER'S FLOWER GARDEN; 78" x 86"; hexagons are variegated prints & solids set in soft green with white lining; 50/50 cotton & poly blends; made in Kentucky in 1989; hand pieced & quilted; polyester batting, scalloped sides. $230.00

7140391

1150391

2150391

3150391

4150391

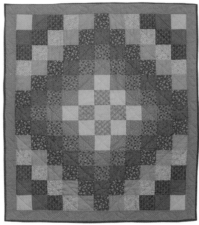

5150391

6150391

7150391

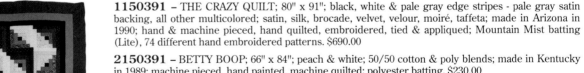

1150391 – THE CRAZY QUILT; 80" x 91"; black, white & pale gray edge stripes - pale gray satin backing, all other multicolored; satin, silk, brocade, velvet, velour, moiré, taffeta; made in Arizona in 1990; hand & machine pieced, hand quilted, embroidered, tied & appliqued; Mountain Mist batting (Lite), 74 different hand embroidered patterns. $690.00

2150391 – BETTY BOOP; 66" x 84"; peach & white; 50/50 cotton & poly blends; made in Kentucky in 1989; machine pieced, hand painted, machine quilted; polyester batting. $230.00

3150391 – MICHIGAN-CHERRY CAPITOL OF THE WORLD; 80" x 101"; burgundy, rust, red cherries, dark & light gray leaves, ivory background & backing; all cotton; made in Michigan in 1990; hand appliqued, embroidered & quilted; polyester batting, rod pocket on back, scalloped edge. $629.00

4150391 – LONE STAR; 92" x 98"; pastel solids, light blue, pink, yellow & creams on off-white background; cottons, cotton-polys; made in Virginia in 1990; machine pieced, hand quilted; thin-bonded poly batting, pastel floral backing with wide light blue border on back, quilted around every piece (double quilting on star pieces), dated. $322.00

5150391 – TRIP AROUND THE WORLD; 40" x 47"; pastel prints with light blue border, mint green print backing with colonial blue binding; 100% cotton; made in Georgia in 1990; machine pieced, hand quilted; polyester batting. $92.00

6150391 – LOVER'S KNOT; 90" x 100"; coral, aqua, teal, white/coral print; 100% cotton, pre-washed; made in New York in 1990; machine pieced, hand quilted; Fairfield Traditional polyester batting, Log Cabin variation forms knots across surface, colored thread used in quilting gives added depth to design. $690.00

7150391 – LOG CABIN; 81" x 104"; blue; cotton; made in Kentucky in 1990; machine pieced, hand quilted. $345.00

1160391

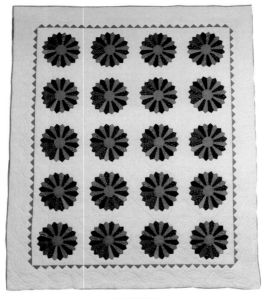

2160391

3160391

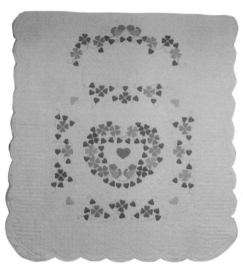

4160391

5160391

6160391

1160391 – LOG CABIN; 42" x 58"; blue, rose & cream; poly/cotton blend; made in Ohio in 1990; machine pieced, hand quilted; poly batting. $173.00

2160391 – DRESDEN PLATE; 88" x 106"; solid medium blue, blue prints on white background; cotton - cotton poly; made in New York in 1989; machine & hand pieced, hand quilted; poly batting. $403.00

3160391 – WEDDING RING; 84" x 101"; wine, green on yellow background; made in Illinois in 1989; hand pieced & embroidered; polyester batting, scalloped edges. $334.00

4160391 – COUNTRY SWEETHEART; 97" x 110"; off-white, peach & green; poly cotton, 100% cotton; made in Missouri in 1990; hand embroidered, appliqued & quilted; polyester batting, large hearts in center, all leaves & flower petals are heart shaped. $661.00

5160391 – SCRAP HAPPY SAMPLER; 42" x 42"; multicolored scraps on sky blue background; 100% cottons; made in New Hampshire in 1990; hand & machine pieced, hand appliqued & quilted; low loft batting. $288.00

6160391 – DRESDEN PLATE; 67" x 86"; multicolor on white blocks with pink borders; cotton; machine pieced, hand appliqued & quilted. $380.00

7160391 – 9 PATCH/SPIKEY & PEAK; 42" x 42"; bright southwestern pinks, turquoise, earth tones; cotton; made in Texas in 1990; machine pieced; poly batting, bright 2 block wallhanging with original quilting design. $207.00

7160391

94

1170391

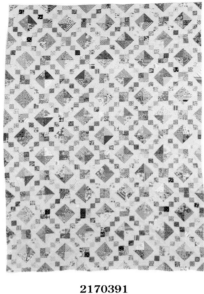

2170391

3170391

4170391

5170391

6170391

7170391

1170391 – SAW; 84" x 92"; muslin, brown, 2 shades muted pink, 2 shades green; 100% cotton face; made in New York in 1990; machine pieced; poly batting, poly/cotton percale backing, medallion quilt with quilted motifs of leaves, butterflies & flowers. $575.00

2170391 – SINGLE IRISH CHAIN VARIATION; 66" x 94"; multicolored on yellow background & border; cotton; top made c. 1940, quilted c. 1960 in Kansas; machine pieced, hand quilted; cotton flannel batting, colorful prints from 1920's, 30's & 40's, backing is large flower printed sheet. $230.00

3170391 – LOG CABIN; 89" x 101"; forest green & light green; poly & cotton, VIP calico; made in Illinois in 1990; machine pieced & quilted; bonded poly batting, matching print for lining, binding is double & double stitched. $230.00

4170391 – LOG CABIN STAR; 92" x 106"; blue & blue green with off-white background; poly/cotton; made in Ohio in 1990; machine pieced, hand quilted; polyester batting. $460.00

5170391 – SOFT DREAMS; 79" x 92"; tan & prints; 100% cotton; made in Wisconsin; machine pieced, hand quilted; 2 matching ruffled pillow shams included. $275.00

6170391 – FOUR PATCH CHAIN; 82" x 100"; blue/navy/white; 100% cotton; made in Wisconsin in 1990; machine pieced, hand quilted; polyester batting, navy print backing. $259.00

7170391 – BISCUIT QUILT; 54½" x 69"; light blue, paisley background; polished cotton, tie silk & poly; made in Idaho in 1990; no batting. $518.00

95

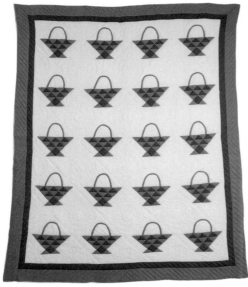

1180391

2180391

3180391

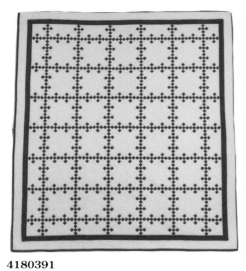

4180391

5180391

6180391

1180391 – BASKET QUILT; 71" x 91½"; salmon & teal baskets on white background; cotton; made in Texas in 1990; hand pieced; cotton batting. $345.00

2180391 – TRIP AROUND THE WORLD; 40" x 48"; rose pink, blue, off-white prints; all 100% cotton; made in Illinois in 1990; machine pieced, hand quilted; Fairfield Traditional Batting, backing is solid rose pink 100% cotton fabric. $136.00

3180391 – UNKNOWN; 97" x 103"; rose & blue; cotton; made in 1990; machine pieced & quilted. $259.00

4180391 – NINE PATCH OF NINE PATCHES; 86" x 98"; red on white; 100% cotton; made in Illinois in 1989; machine pieced, hand quilted; polyester batting. $460.00

5180391 – LOG CABIN; 34" x 34"; browns & rust; cotton & poly; made in Illinois in 1990; machine pieced, hand quilted. $86.00

6180391 – RAIL FENCE; 94" x 110"; multicolor, rust, orange, light blue with brown backing; polyester/cotton; made in Illinois in 1990; machine pieced, hand quilted; Dacron polyester batting. $201.00

7180391 – EMBROIDERED; 76" x 78"; off-white, cross stitched & embroidered in blue, green, lavender with pink binding; cotton; made in Ohio c. 1920; hand quilted & embroidered; few small age spots, flannel batting. $150.00

7180391

1190391

2190391

3190391

4190391

5190391

6190391

7190391

1190391 – LOG CABIN; 26" x 35½"; mauves, pinks & blues; cotton, cotton blends; made in Nebraska in 1990; machine pieced, hand quilted; polyfil. $60.00

2190391 – PLAIN JANE; 94" x 94"; white & turkey red on white muslin backing; 100% cotton; made in Pennsylvania in 1990; machine pieced, hand quilted; poly batting, bias binding, some pencil markings show, quilting in 1½" squares. $805.00

3190391 – UNKNOWN; 44" x 44"; multicolored hearts on white background; cotton, blends; made in Texas in 1989; machine pieced & appliqued, hand quilted. $115.00

4190391 – STARS & HEARTS; 86" x 100"; shades of rose & slate blue; all cotton top with poly cotton backing & batting; made in Kansas in 1984; machine pieced, hand quilted; mitered corners, signed & dated. $500.00

5190391 – SOLID PLAIN; 44" x 60"; unbleached muslin on one side with light blue print on the other; cotton polyester; made in Illinois in 1990; hand quilted; Dacron polyester batting; reversible. $60.00

6190391 – IRISH CHAIN; 81" x 98"; blue & white with striped slate blue bows; all cotton; made in Kansas in 1990; machine pieced, hand appliqued & quilted; polyfill batting, cotton poly lining, mitered corners, double bias, signed & dated. $489.00

7190391 – WINDMILL; 85" x 98"; cream & 3 shades of peach prints; cotton poly blend; made in Montana in 1990; machine pieced, hand quilted; medium weight polyester batting. $385.00

97

1010691

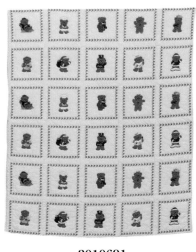

2010691

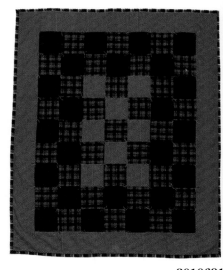

3010691

4010691

5010691

6010691

7010691

1010691 – DOUBLE STAR or MOSAIC TILE; 80" x 84"; red & white; cotton; top made in 1925, completed in 1987; hand pieced & quilted; polyester low-loft batting. $403.00

2010691 – X-MAS PRINT; 36" x 45"; beige, reds & greens; cotton poly; made in Montana in 1990; hand quilted; lap quilt or wallhanging, poly batting. $55.00

3010691 – ALTERNATING BLOCK PATTERN; 77" x 96"; hot pink, turquoise blue & black; top is poly wool blend & back is matching cotton flannel; made in Ohio in 1990; machine pieced, tied; hand bound & tied with matching yarn, mitered corners, poly blanket batting, hanging sleeve. $288.00

4010691 – LOVE RING; 45" x 45"; dark & light blue prints; cotton blends; made in Nebraska in 1990; machine pieced, hand quilted; polyfil. $104.00

5010691 – UNTITLED; 28" x 34"; Amish colors, black with bright solids; cotton; made in Texas in 1990; machine pieced, hand quilted; poly batting, wallhanging of black triangles & solid triangles, one blue border, one black border, blue binding, hanging sleeve. $115.00

6010691 – CIRCLE OF DOVES; 27" x 27"; peach & brown with brown print; cotton/poly blend; made in Ozarks in 1987; hand pieced & quilted; prairie point border. $60.00

7010691 – EIGHT POINTED STARS; 54" x 54"; navy, old tan, antique gold, dusty rose; 100% cottons; made in Virginia in 1990; machine pieced, hand quilted; flowers positioned to form a circle & wreath inside stars, bonded poly batting, solid tan backing, double bias bound, signed & dated. $173.00

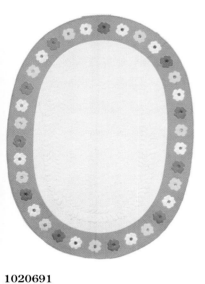

1020691

2020691

3020691

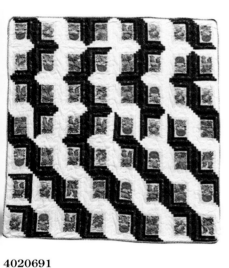

4020691

5020691

6020691

1020691 – OVAL TABLECLOTH; 57" x 76"; beige top, light brown drop around table, flowers are shades of yellow & orange; cotton & cotton blends; made in 1983; hand appliqued & quilted; polyester bonded batting, background quilting is ½" apart. $225.00

2020691 – LOG CABIN/LONE STAR; 112" x 112"; red, white & blue; cotton, poly & combinations; made in New Hampshire & Florida in 1990; machine pieced, hand quilted; Mountain Mist batting. $805.00

3020691 – IRIS; 81" x 94"; white percale, purple, pink, orchids, yellow, red & green leaves & stems; prints; made in Indiana in 1990; hand pieced, appliqued & quilted; polyester filler. $1,150.00

4020691 – VARIATION OF LOG CABIN; 90" x 96"; navy blue & off-white; cotton & poly; made in California in 1990; machine pieced & quilted; 100% poly batting. $173.00

5020691 – HEXAGONS SET IN SHAPE OF DIAMONDS; 70" x 89"; red with multicolors; cottons; made in Nebraska ca. 1950; hand pieced & quilted; poly batting, background is mostly red with some cream at each end & binding, multicolored fabrics in hexagons that represent flowers. $322.00

6020691 – LOG CABIN STAR; 86" x 100"; shades of blue with touch of pastel colors (mostly rose); all cotton top; made in Kansas in 1990; machine pieced, hand quilted; cotton poly & polyester batting, double binding, mitered corners, signed & dated. $489.00

7020691 – EAGLE; 41" x 41"; blue, white dots center, red background; cotton & poly-cotton; made in Wisconsin in 1991; hand appliqued & embroidered, machine pieced & quilted; polyester batting. $87.00

7020691

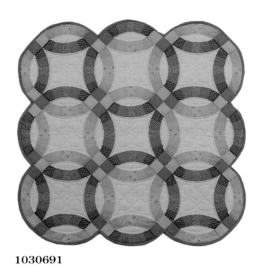

1030691

2030691

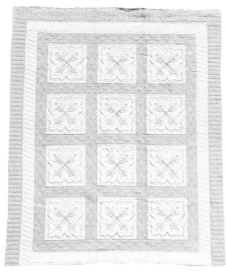

3030691

4030691

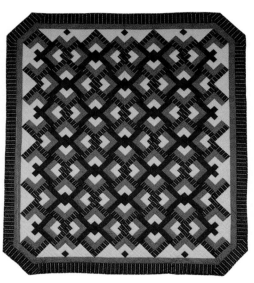

5030691

6030691

7030691

1030691 – DOUBLE WEDDING RING; 44" x 44"; peach & seafoam green with off-white background; poly/cotton; made in Missouri in 1989; machine pieced, hand quilted; dacron batting, Mennonite made, hearts quilting design, loops for hanging, signed & dated. $104.00

2030691 – BASKET OF LILIES; 79" x 96"; pink & green with small pink flowers on white background; all cottons; made in New York in 1986; machine pieced, hand appliqued & quilted; bonded polyester batting. $1,265.00

3030691 – TULIPS; 85" x 96"; pink tulips outlined in medium blue with off-white background; cotton; made in Illinois in 1989; hand embroidered & quilted. $345.00

4030691 – CHAINED STARS (LeMoyne Star & Irish Chain); 46" x 46"; slate blue & peach on white print background; 100% cotton; made in Kentucky in 1991; hand & machine pieced, hand quilted; polyfil traditional batting. $202.00

5030691 – LOVER'S KNOT; 94" x 104"; wine, dull aqua green, cream; cotton, cotton blends; made in Nebraska in 1989; machine pieced, hand quilted; polyfill batting. $345.00

6030691 – DIAMONDS ARE FOREVER; 72" x 87"; mauve & tan on cream background; 100% cotton top & back; made in Pennsylvania in 1990; hand appliqued hearts, machine pieced, hand quilted; Mountain Mist batting, original design, quilted with many hearts & flowing lines, signed & dated. $391.00

7030691 – TULIP BALLET; 92" x 104"; multicolor tulips; perma-press; made in California in 1990; hand stitched except to sew blocks & borders strips together; Mountain Mist batting - dacron polyester. $489.00

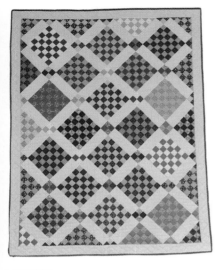

1040691

2040691

3040691

4040691

5040691

6040691

1040691 – GRANDMOTHER'S PRIDE; 74" x 96"; rich blues & green set against wheat; 100% pre-washed cotton; made in Illinois in 1990; machine pieced, hand quilted. $368.00

2040691 – COLOR CRAYONS; 37" x 55"; multicolor & white; cotton; made in New Mexico in 1990; machine pieced & quilted; Mountain Mist polyester batting. $65.00

3040691 – FEATHER FLOWERS; 26½" x 26½"; cranberry, navy & off-white; cotton, cotton & polyester; made in Minnesota in 1990; hand appliqued & quilted; polyester batting, adaptation of an old applique pattern, has hanging sleeve. $70.00

4040691 – DOUBLE IRISH CHAIN; 84" x 104"; medium soft green with touch of rose & blue; all cotton; made in Kansas in 1990; machine pieced, hand quilted; poly cotton backing & batting, double bias binding, mitered corners, signed & dated. $483.00

5040691 – SHIMMERING STARS; 25" x 25"; blues & burgundys; 100% cotton; quilted in Tennessee in 1987; hand pieced & quilted; cotton fabric with different stripes was chosen to design all star, a design in each star, change of value in the background to create visual interest, Mountain Mist regular batting. $127.00

6040691 – DRESDEN PLATE; 76" x 91"; tiny flowered blues on pale blue background; blends & cotton; made in Arkansas in 1988; machine pieced & appliqued, hand quilted; 16 petals in each block, navy to light blue tiny flowers, 4 solid blue petals in each plate, light blue background & backing, double bias binding, polyester batting. $230.00

7040691 – TARTAN PLAID; 33" x 33"; tan, cream, red, navy, med. blues; cotton; made in Minnesota in 1991; machine pieced, hand quilted; Polyester batting, two-block quilt using a border print. $195.00

7040691

101

1050691

2050691

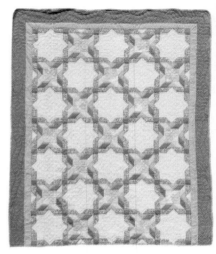

3050691

4050691

5050691

6050691

7050691

1050691 – DRUNKARD'S PATH; 86" x 94"; red on white; cotton; made in Illinois in 1991; machine pieced, hand quilted; polyester batting. $288.00

2050691 – PATRIOTIC SQUARES; 35" x 40"; red & blue prints; cotton & blends; made in North Carolina in 1991; machine pieced & quilted; red & blue 1½" squares & muslin, diagonal machine quilting, border with squares on point, polyester batting, signed & dated. $98.00

3050691 – CACTUS FLOWER; 84" x 102"; pink, green & unbleached muslin & tan print; all cotton; made in Nevada in 1991; machine pieced, hand quilted; Hobbs batting. $460.00

4050691 – LOON SUNSET; 65" x 93"; light, bright rosy colors with dark blues & greens, reverses to deep blue; cotton & blends; made in Massachusetts in 1990; machine pieced, hand appliqued & quilted; polyfil batting, loon has red bead eye. $345.00

5050691 – WREATHED STAR; 93" x 116"; blue, brown & off-white; poly/cotton; made in Ohio in 1990; machine pieced, hand quilted; poly batting, acorns & oak leaves quilted in corners. $575.00

6050691 – UPTOWN DISTRICT; 82" x 102"; burgundy, terra cotta, teal; cotton; made in California in 1991; machine pieced & quilted; Cotton Classic batting, quilted in Waves pattern by Shirley Greenhoe. $633.00

7050691 – 8-POINT STAR; 44" x 44"; burgundy, rose & colonial blue; cotton/polyester blend; made in Kentucky in 1991; machine pieced, hand quilted; polyester batting. $190.00

1060691

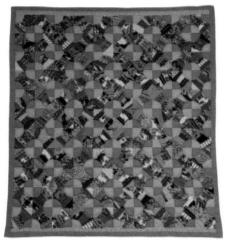

2060691

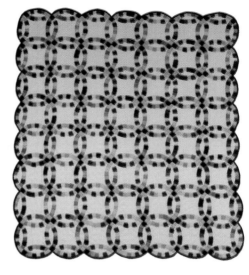

3060691

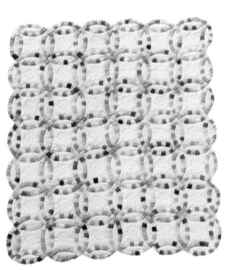

4060691

5060691

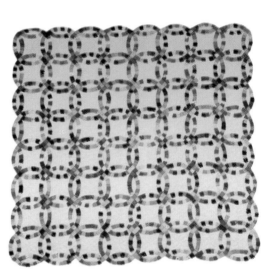

6060691

1060691 – FEATHERED STAR; 54" x 54"; red & black prints with antique tea-dyed background; 100% cotton designer fabrics; made in Delaware in 1991; machine pieced, hand quilted; quilted heart & feathered designs, has outline quilting, polyester batting, double fabric binding, natural color cotton backing. $403.00

2060691 – STRING SNOWBALL; 75½" x 85"; pink & beige; cotton; age of antique quilt top unknown, finished & quilted in 1989; hand pieced & quilted; polyester batting. $317.00

3060691 – DOUBLE WEDDING RING; 90" x 102"; multicolor; cotton; made in Kentucky in 1990; machine pieced, hand quilted; Mountain Mist batting. $374.00

4060691 – DOUBLE WEDDING RING; 78" x 92"; purple; cotton/polyester; made in Missouri in 1990; machine pieced, hand quilted; polyester batting. $345.00

5060691 – ROLLING STONES WHEEL; 62" x 86"; gold, red, pink & blue; cotton (feed sacks); made in New York ca. 1940; hand & machine pieced, hand quilted; cotton batting, colorful scrap quilt. $380.00

6060691 – DOUBLE WEDDING RING; 98" x 98"; scrap quilt with off-white background; cotton & cotton blends; made in Missouri in 1986; machine pieced, hand quilted; polyester batting. $300.00

7060691 – "POLINAHE" ANTHURIUM; 39" x 39"; red & dusty rose with calico backing; Imperial broadcloth, 60-40 poly/cotton blend, 100% cotton calico; made in Marshall Islands in 1990; hand appliqued & quilted; Mountain Mist polyester batting, Hawaiian quilt with rows of quilting ½" apart, anthurium design quilted in border. $242.00

7060691

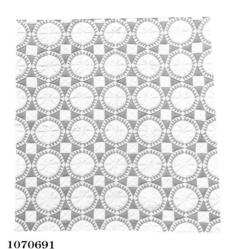

1070691

2070691

3070691

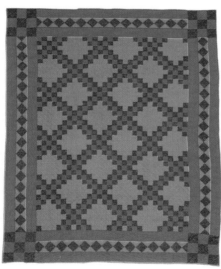

4070691

5070691

6070691

7070691

1070691 – INDIAN SUMMER; 72" x 78"; cream muslin, burnt orange; 100% cotton; made in North Carolina ca. 1920's; hand pieced, hand quilted; renovated & finished, few minor trunk stains, tiny quilting stitches, muslin backing, bias bound. $345.00

2070691 – UNTITLED; 75" x 77"; multicolor, solids & prints, solid pink & white borders with pink backing; cottons; assembled in New York in 1990; hand & machine pieced, hand quilted; poly batting, new except for "old" blocks. $374.00

3070691 – PIONEER LOG CABIN; 76" x 88"; red, white & blue; cotton-polyester blends; made in Idaho in 1988; machine pieced, hand quilted; Mountain Mist polyester batting, signed & dated. $161.00

4070691 – IRISH CHAIN; 83" x 101"; burgundy, blue-green & navy; cotton; made in Kentucky in 1990; machine pieced, hand quilted; 100% polyester batting. $403.00

5070691 – LOG CABIN FAN; 86" x 99"; shades of blue & white; cotton front & poly & cotton backing; made in Kansas in 1989; machine pieced, hand quilted; Mountain Mist batting, fan quilted in each corner of fan block, mitered corners, double binding, signed & dated. $472.00

6070691 – GRANDMOTHER'S FLOWER GARDEN; 72" x 84"; light green background with white paths & multicolored flowers; cotton & cotton/polyester blend; made in Arkansas in 1990; hand pieced & quilted; thin polyester batting, has quilted flower designs around border, white fabric for backing & binding. $253.00

7070691 – PURPLE LOVER; 58" x 58"; multicolored Amish solid baskets with black background, deep aubergine purple border, hunter green backing; cotton & cotton/poly blends; made in Colorado in 1991; machine pieced, hand quilted; Hobbs poly-down black batting, original design, signed & dated. $345.00

1080691

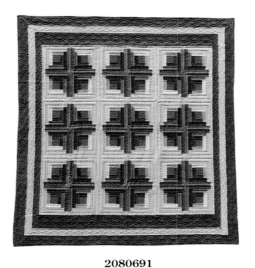

2080691

3080691

4080691

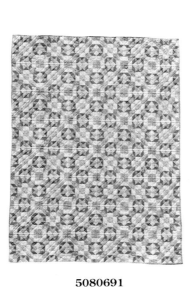

5080691

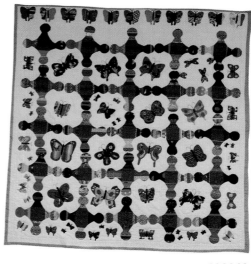

6080691

1080691 – PUCKER PATCH ROSE; 42" x 42"; mauve & off-white shadow print; cotton/poly; made in Illinois in 1990; hand appliqued & quilted; has hearts & flowers in quilting design. $213.00

2080691 – LOG CABIN VARIATION; 92" x 100"; primarily blues with touches of dull red, some white & cream background; cotton-cotton blends; made in Nebraska in 1990; machine pieced, hand quilted; polyfil batting. $397.00

3080691 – LOG CABIN BARN RAISING; 44" x 44"; pinks, blues & lavenders with a cream border; 100% cotton; made in Georgia in 1990; machine pieced, hand quilted; Hobbs polyester batting, Amish pattern, has hanging sleeve. $276.00

4080691 – TRIP AROUND THE WORLD; 84" x 93"; light to medium prints & solids, light wine lining; cotton; made in Alabama in 1989; machine pieced, hand quilted; poly batting, double quilted. $345.00

5080691 – FRIENDSHIP STAR; 64" x 86"; white & cream muslin, light purple solid & prints, light green prints, back & binding light purple; cotton; made in Illinois; hand pieced & quilted; each 10½" block contains 57 pieces. $460.00

6080691 – A BUTTERFLY AT NIGHT; 102" x 105"; variety of colors with off-white background; cotton; made in Kentucky in 1984; hand quilted; polyester batting, patterns of butterflies in all shapes & sizes surrounded by piecework with border of butterflies at top. $1,380.00

7080691 – TULIPS IN BLOOM; 95" x 106"; forest green, blues & white; cotton, cotton/poly; made in Ohio in 1990; hand appliqued & quilted; polyester batting, quilted with designs of flowers, stems, leaves, vines, hearts, neatly hand bound with double fabric. $518.00

7080691

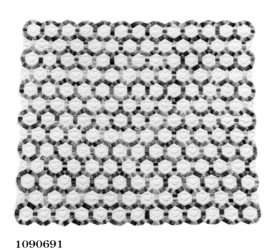

1090691

2090691

3090691

4090691

5090691

6090691

7090691

1090691 – FRIENDSHIP RING; 81" x 92"; white background with blue, pink & various prints; cotton, cotton-poly; made in Arkansas in 1990; hand pieced & quilted; polyester batting. $259.00

2090691 – GIANT DAHLIA; 64" x 86"; mauve, pink, blue, navy with ecru background; cotton, cotton blends; made in Nebraska in 1991; machine pieced, hand quilted; polyfil batting, lots of quilting. $386.00

3090691 – COUNTRY PATCH; 64" x 80"; multicolors set in paths of white; soft polyester knit; made in Kentucky in 1988; hand pieced & quilted; Mountain Mist batting, white lining, deep scalloped sides. $173.00

4090691 – KALEIDOSCOPE/KEY WEST BEAUTY; 71" x 91"; pastel & bright prints & solids on off-white background; mostly cotton with few poly-cotton fabrics; made in Illinois in 1986; machine pieced, hand quilted; Fairfield cotton classic batting, backing is light beige 100% cotton. $805.00

5090691 – SQUAW QUILT; 88" x 105"; prints/desert sand; cotton; made in Arkansas in 1991; hand appliqued & quilted; polyfil batting, has ribbon & yarn braids, signed & dated. $460.00

6090691 – NINE PATCH JEWEL BOX; 70" x 82"; blue, deep lavender, black; 100% cotton; made in North Dakota in 1991; machine pieced & quilted, Mountain Mist poly batting, started with red & blue madras (that started as a stripe) 2½" 9-patches & simply grew from there. $334.00

7090691 – VARIABLE STAR; 88" x 104"; pink on white print background & backing, shades of pink; 100% cottons; made in New York in 1990; machine pieced, hand quilted; polyester batting, signed & dated. $460.00

1100691

2100691

3100691

4100691

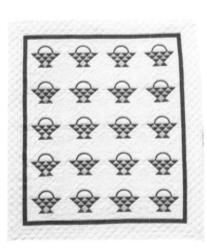

5100691

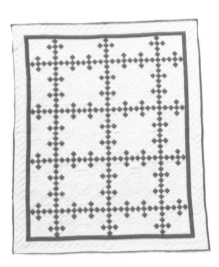

6100691

1100691 – PENNSYLVANIA DUTCH CROSS STITCH; 84" x 95"; white with embroidery colors of rose & pink shades; cotton; made in Colorado ca. 1980; cross stitch, hand quilted; embroidery of hearts, flowers & birds, made from commercial kit, some pre-printed marking dots for quilting are visible, polyester batting. $391.00

2100691 – CORNER STONE LOG CABIN; 81" x 99"; blue; cotton/polyester; made in Missouri; machine pieced, hand quilted; polyester batting. $403.00

3100691 – TRIP AROUND THE WORLD; 78" x 94"; various blues & white; cottons & cotton/poly blends; made in Kentucky in 1990; hand pieced, machine quilted; loop design, polyester batting, tie dyed lining, bias binding. $202.00

4100691 – WHIRLIGIG or WINDING WAYS; 83" x 93"; shades of blue; cotton, cotton/poly blends; made in Illinois in 1989; machine pieced & quilted; poly batting, quilted in rose pattern, pattern of top gives changing illusions of circles overlapping. $156.00

5100691 – FRUIT BASKET; 88" x 106"; off-white, medium blue, medium blue on off-white prints; cotton, cotton-poly; made in New York in 1989; machine pieced, hand appliqued & quilted; poly batting. $403.00

6100691 – DOUBLE NINE-PATCH; 80" x 100"; red & off-white; all cotton; made in Connecticut in 1988; machine pieced, hand quilted; polyester batting, floral white muslin print backing, binding is double layer red on white print. $598.00

7100691 – SEA & SHADOWS; 71" x 84"; blue, brown, cream; cotton & cotton blends; made in Iowa in 1987; hand pieced & quilted; Mountain Mist batting, a Sandra Hatch pattern. $518.00

7100691

107

1110691

2110691

3110691

4110691

5110691

6110691

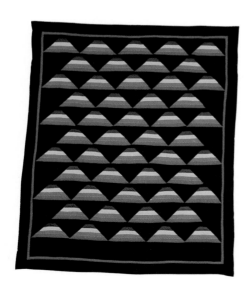

7110691

1110691 – OHIO STAR; 85" x 96"; navy & white; cotton; made in Texas in 1990; machine pieced, hand quilted; Mountain Mist batting, feather wreath quilting in plain blocks. $345.00

2110691 – NINE-PATCH; 78" x 89"; blue, burgundy, off-white background, green border; mostly cottons, some polyesters; made in California in 1991; machine pieced, hand quilted; Mountain Mist polyester batting, signed & dated. $288.00

3110691 – RADIANT STAR; 88" x 103"; light to dark blues with white backround & backing; cotton/polyester blends; made in Illinois in 1991; machine pieced, hand quilted; dacron batting, signed & dated. $460.00

4110691 – TRIP AROUND THE WORLD; 86" x 100"; roses & blues, prints & solids, blue print back; all cotton; made in Pennsylvania in 1991; machine pieced, hand quilted; bonded polyester batting. $403.00

5110691 – MIDNIGHT STAR; 82" x 94"; light & dark blue prints, beige prints; 100% cotton; made in Maine in 1990; machine pieced, hand quilted; Mountain Mist polyester batting, single piece muslin back, hanging sleeve, signed & dated. $288.00

6110691 – UNTITLED; 61½" x 75"; pink, gray & black; all cottons; made in Georgia in 1986; hand appliqued, hand quilted, final assembly by machine; Mountain Mist regular batting, alternate pink & gray blocks with black print tape (self made), black border. $173.00

7110691 – STRIPES AND STARS; 75" x 80"; black, turquoise, pink, yellow & purple; cotton-poly; made in Arizona in 1991; hand quilted; Mountain Mist poly batting, stripes double quilted, triangles quilted with stars. $460.00

1120691

2120691

3120691

4120691

5120691

6120691

1120691 – TENNESSEE WALTZ; 86" x 104"; burgundy, black, tan; 100% cotton; made in Illinois in 1990; machine pieced, hand quilted; Mountain Mist batting. $518.00

2120691 – AMISH SHADOWS; 66" x 86"; black/purple; 100% cotton; made in 1990, machine pieced, hand quilted; Mountain Mist Quilt Light batting. $270.00

3120691 – UNTITLED; 79" x 90"; pinks & green; cotton & polyester blend; made in Illinois in 1991; machine pieced, hand embroidered & quilted; extra thick batting, quilted in a design to give it a puffy look. $345.00

4120691 – BOWTIE; 80" x 88"; green & blue with green backing; cotton; made in Louisiana; machine pieced, hand quilted; possibly blanket batting, quilt material is hospital "scrubs" from quilt-maker's husband's internship. $196.00

5120691 – TURKEY TRACKS; 80" x 92"; red & white; cotton & polyester blend; made in 1989; hand quilted; polyester batting. $518.00

6120691 – PRESIDENT'S WREATH; 84" x 88"; green wreaths with pink flowers & yellow centers, white background; cotton; made in 1930's-40's; hand appliqued & quilted; applique done in soft pastels, overall quilting in diagonal lines & triple cables, enhanced by a triple border, slight discoloration of green wreaths in several places. $374.00

7120691 – ARROW LOG CABIN; 84" x 96"; shades of light & dark rust; poly-cotton blends; made in Illinois in 1988; machine pieced & quilted; Hobbs Bonded Poly batting, off-white lining, double binding & double stitched, variation of Log Cabin set in arrow pattern. $173.00

7120691

1130691

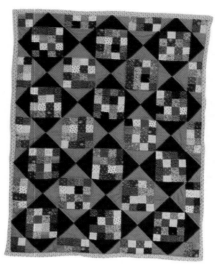

2130691

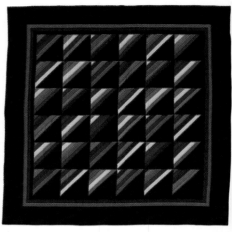

3130691

4130691

5130691

6130691

7130691

1130691 – CORNERS IN THE CABINS; 24½" x 24½"; charcoal, aqua greens, mauve accent, white background; 100% cottons; made in Nebraska in 1989; machine pieced, hand quilted; polyfill batting, triangle pieces are incorporated with a unique technique which leaves the long edge free, frequently called "toe-catchers," has hanging sleeve. $144.00

2130691 – ROAD TO SAINT LOUIS; 35" x 44"; brown & tan; 100% cottons, some cotton/poly; made in California in 1991; machine pieced & quilted; Mountain Mist polyester batting, brown & tan setting triangles give all the colors order. $110.00

3130691 – AMISH SHADOWS WALL QUILT; 56" x 56"; black with red, purple, royal blue, yellow, copper & tan; 100% cotton; made in Illinois in 1991; machine pieced, hand quilted; Hobbs Poly-Down batting, black backing, has rod pocket, lot of detailed quilting, feather pattern quilted in border, signed & dated. $575.00

4130691 – DIAMOND WONDER; 35"; teal blue, rose, deep blue; 100% cotton; made in New Hampshire in 1991; machine pieced, hand quilted; color study in predominantly teal blues, unique hexagon shape, hand quilting highlights each diamond facet, original, signed & dated. $115.00

5130691 – SCHOOL HOUSE; 42" x 56"; peach & mint green; 100% cotton; made in Indiana in 1991; hand pieced & quilted; polyester batting, "Nap Size" quilt, white backing, signed & dated. $167.00

6130691 – STAR TWIST; 48½" x 48½"; black floral print with rose & blue, muslin background; 100% cotton; made in Connecticut in 1991; hand & machine pieced, hand quilted; Mountain Mist polyester batting, signed & dated. $230.00

7130691 – STAR OF THE EAST (based on Evening Star block); 35" x 46½"; blue, burgundy & rose; background is white with tiny rose figure; 100% cotton; made in North Carolina in 1990; machine pieced, hand quilted; interesting print fabrics & unusual set lend an Oriental feel to this block, crosshatching, feathers, wreaths, bound & backed in burgundy print, signed & dated, hanging sleeve. $213.00

110

1140691

2140691

3140691

4140691

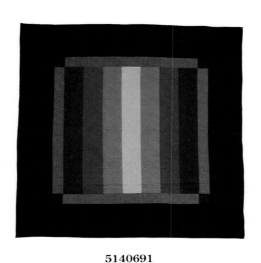

5140691

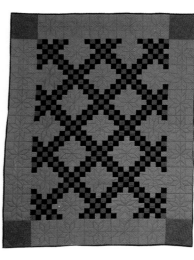

6140691

1140691 – GRANDMOTHER'S FLOWER GARDEN; 90" x 108" before quilting; blue & green; poly-cotton muslin; made in Missouri in 1990; machine pieced, hand quilted, polyester batting, regular quilt lining, quilted piece by piece, signed & dated. $345.00

2140691 – GIANT DAHLIA; 108" x 113"; navy, cream, burgundy, rose, blue; 100% cotton; made in Indiana in 1989; machine pieced, hand pieced, hand quilted; 100% polyester batting, quilted by Amish lady, lots of feather quilting. $892.00

3140691 – SOUTHWEST I; 53½" x 41½"; peach background, rose, turquoise, black with rose back-ing; 100% cotton; made in Virginia in 1990; machine pieced, hand quilted; Mountain Mist Low Loft poly batting, has hanging sleeve. $150.00

4140691 – SUMMER FLOWERS; 86" x 102"; white background with red, blue, yellow, green calico appliques; cotton; made in Montana in 1986; machine appliqued & quilted; polyester batting, one flower appliqued to block with plain squares that alternate, set together with sashing. $460.00

5140691 – AMISH BARS; 96" x 96"; dark gray, black, purples, olive, turquoise, beige; 100% cotton; made in Massachusetts in 1988; machine pieced, hand quilted; handmade bias binding, black back, Mountain Mist poly batting, signed & dated. $518.00

6140691 – DOUBLE IRISH CHAIN; 67" x 87"; gray, black & teal; 100% cottons; made in Colorado in 1987; machine pieced, hand quilted; poly batting, quilted with stars in open blocks & border, baskets in corner, has one tiny mend in one star. $345.00

7140691 – SINGLE WEDDING RING; 84" x 97½"; white on off-white floral muslin, cranberry rose, deep green floral; 100% cotton; made in New York in 1991; machine pieced, free-motion machine quilted; Mountain Mist poly batting, has hearts & flower-like motifs quilted in borders & white blocks, coordi-nating cotton floral backing. $518.00

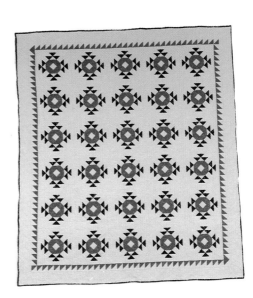

7140691

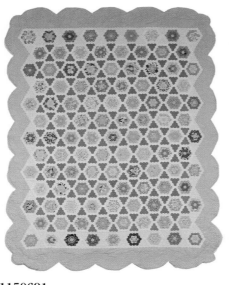

1150691

2150691

3150691

4150691

5150691

6150691

7150691

1150691 – GRANDMOTHER'S FLOWER GARDEN; 92" x 120"; multicolored scrap fabrics with green with pink backing, outside border & binding; 100% cottons; quilted in Nebraska in 1990; hand pieced & quilted; polyester batting, antique quilt top from the 30's, top flowers are outline quilted, border is stencil quilted with flowers, leaves & bows at corners. $920.00

2150691 – LOVER'S KNOT; 92" x 104"; light rose, colonial blue, shades of blue & rose on navy background, light rose & colonial blue on white background; 100% cotton; made in Pennsylvania in 1990; machine pieced, hand quilted; Mountain Mist 100% polyester batting. $805.00

3150691 – FAN; 37" x 47"; greens & peach on black with peach backing; all cotton; made in South Carolina in 1990; machine pieced & quilted; Mountain Mist poly batting. $75.00

4150691 – GRAPEVINES; 89" x 105"; green vines, purple grapes on beige background; cotton; made in Pennsylvania in 1977; machine pieced, hand embroidered, appliqued & quilted, hand trapuntoed grapes; Mountain Mist batting, grapes & vines are echo hand quilted. $685.00

5150691 – SUNSHINE & SHADOW; 94" x 102"; blues, greens, reds, purples with a black border; broadcloth; made in Maine in 1989; machine pieced, hand quilted; poly batting, flower stencil border. $575.00

6150691 – LOG CABIN; 83" x 99"; scrap with a print lining & blue binding; cotton; made in Alabama in 1990; machine pieced & quilted; polyester batting, has variable star in center with barn raising diamond. $575.00

7150691 – KALEIDOSCOPE; 78" x 90"; white, red print, navy print, dark navy backing; cotton blends; made in Virginia in 1982; machine pieced, hand quilted; polyfil traditional batting, new fabrics, signed & dated. $403.00

112

1160691

2160691

3160691

4160691

5160691

6160691

1160691 – TRIPLE IRISH CHAIN; 90" x 110"; colonial blue prints with natural muslin background; 100% cotton; made in California in 1990; machine pieced, hand quilted; 12-14 stitches per inch, bonded polyester batting. $690.00

2160691 – 3-D PINE TREE; 86" x 103"; green print/unbleached muslin; 100% cotton; made in Virginia in 1982; machine pieced, hand quilted; three dimensional original design of trees constructed using strips and prairie points; prize winner; featured in AQS 1985 Quilt Art Engagement Calendar. $2,990.00

3160691 – SAMPLER; 77" x 89"; blue & navy prints, royal blue sash & border, cotton & poly cotton, white muslin background & backing; made in Pennsylvania in 1990; hand pieced or appliqued, sash & border machine sewn, hand quilted; Quilter's Choice polyester traditional batting, quilted with 1" diagonal crosshatching, border has quilted flower & ribbon design, quilted leaf design on sashwork, mitered corners, double handmade matching bias binding, has rod pocket. $978.00

4160691 – FLYING GEESE VARIATION; 92" x 94"; shades of blue & brown with gold & white accents; cotton-poly blend; made in Oklahoma in 1989; machine pieced, hand quilted, some applique; Fairfield poly-fil extra-loft batting. $575.00

5160691 – FLOWER BASKET; 64" x 98"; multicolor prints & solids in fall colors; cottons & blends; made in Mississippi in 1989; hand appliqued & quilted; polyester bonded batting. $345.00

6160691 – INNER SANCTUM; 66" x 66"; black, rust, forest green; 100% cotton; machine pieced, hand quilted, tied; hand & commercially dyed cottons. $488.00

7160691 – GRANDMOTHER'S FLOWER GARDEN; 84" x 97"; teal blue & multicolored flowers on white background & border; cotton; made in Florida in 1988; hand & machine pieced, hand quilted; Mountain Mist Light batting, several flowers are appliqued on back, French fold bias binding scallops the edge, signed & dated. $978.00

7160691

1170691

2170691

3170691

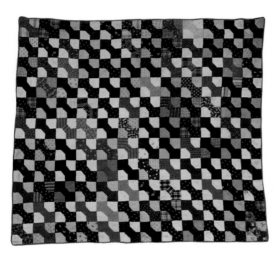

4170691

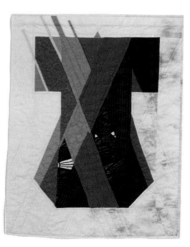

5170691

6170691

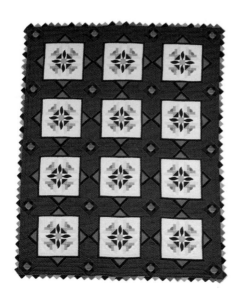

7170691

1170691 – MEDALLION SAMPLER; 71" x 87"; blues, lavenders on white; cottons & cotton blends; made in California in 1988; machine pieced, hand quilted; Mountain Mist regular batting, variety of 10" & 12" blocks border the medallion which contains a 24" block that has been augmented to fit space. $920.00

2170691 – TREE OF LIFE; 78" x 96"; white, blue, yellow, reds & green stem & leaves; prints; made in Indiana in 1989; all handmade & appliqued; polyester batting. $1,150.00

3170691 – SUNFLOWER; 102" x 103"; multicolors, yellow gold & off-white muslin background; cotton, poly cotton & poly; made in Louisiana in 1980; hand quilted; poly cotton backing, black blanket stitch around edge; small spot on lining from ink pin. $259.00

4170691 – BOWTIE; 76" x 85"; multicolored scraps; 100% cottons; made in New York ca. 1900; hand pieced & quilted; some fading on back, lightweight filler. $345.00

5170691 – KIMONO 2; 35" x 47"; pinks, dark red, medium & dark blue, light blue background with mottled gray; Japanese kimono cotton, cotton, cotton/poly; made in California in 1989; machine pieced, machine & hand quilted; bonded poly batting, original design; some fabric strips with raw edges used for accent. $207.00

6170691 – PROMISE OF JUSTICE; 42" x 36"; rainbow pastel solids; cotton; made in Pennsylvania in 1989; machine pieced, hand quilted; polyester batting. $161.00

7170691 – WILD LILY; 80" x 100"; rust, cream, 3 shades peach, green & blue; cotton, some poly/cottons; made in New Jersey in 1989; hand pieced, appliqued & quilted; prairie point edging, polyester batting. $575.00

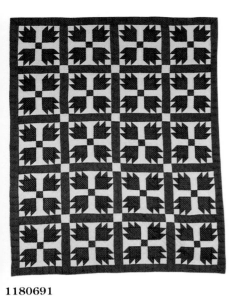

1180691

2180691

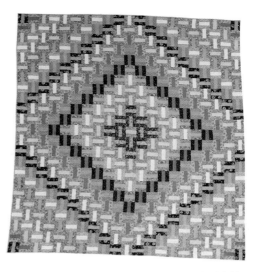

3180691

4180691

5180691

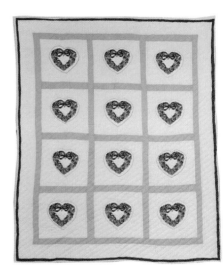

6180691

1180691 – BEAR PAW; 75" x 94"; cream muslin & brown/cream print making paws, plain brown set up & border, white backing & binding; 100% cotton; made in Montana & South Dakota in 1989; machine pieced, hand quilted; Mountain Mist polyester batting. $432.00

2180691 – LOG CABIN (IN BARN RAISING SETTING); 84" x 106"; cream, black, mauve; all 100% cotton; made in Pennsylvania in 1990; machine pieced, hand quilted; quilted ¼" around every log, flowers quilted in border, Fairfield 100% bonded polyester batting, unbleached muslin backing. $633.00

3180691 – RAIL FENCE; 90" x 102"; variety of pastels; cotton top, poly cotton backing; made in Wisconsin in 1990; machine pieced & quilted. $265.00

4180691 – JUDY IN ARABIA; 65" x 75"; black, red & gold; 100% cotton; made in Pennsylvania in 1989; machine pieced, hand quilted; Quilt Light polyester batting, black border surrounding a lighter center gradating out to darker edges, approximately 30 fabrics. $202.00

5180691 – ROCKY MOUNTAIN RAINBOW; 98" x 102"; pink, yellow, lilac, green, blue, cream; 100% cottons; made in Wyoming in 1989; machine pieced & quilted; Mountain Mist 100% polyester batting, quilted in crosshatch design. $299.00

6180691 – HEART QUILT; 71" x 88"; dark blue & pink preprinted roses; polyester; made in New Mexico in 1991; hand quilted; polyester batting. $230.00

7180691 – CLAMSHELL; 74" x 92"; blue, white & varied print; cotton; made in Tennessee in 1989; hand pieced & quilted; polyester batting; muslin sheet lining. $345.00

7180691

1190691

2190691

3190691

4190691

5190691

6190691

7190691

1190691 – JACOB'S LADDER; 80" x 101"; cranberry & beige; cotton prints & plain; made in Illinois in 1990; machine pieced, hand quilted; new quilt from an old pattern. $403.00

2190691 – PINK DRUNKARD'S PATH; 90" x 106"; pink on white background; 50% poly, 50% cotton; made in Missouri in 1989; machine pieced, hand quilted; Mountain Mist batting. $345.00

3190691 – 6 POINT STAR; 88" x 94"; multicolor stars on white background with green, white & yellow border; 100% cotton; made in Iowa in 1988; machine pieced, hand quilted; Mountain Mist batting. $345.00

4190691 – 9-PATCH COUNTRY; 55½" x 71"; blues, rusts, peaches & tans; all cotton; pieced in West Germany, quilted in Florida in 1990; machine pieced & quilted; blue print backing has 35 9-patch blocks in center, making quilt unique & reversible, double fabric, hand stitched binding, polyester batting, has rod pocket & care label with signature. $460.00

5190691 – TUMBLING SQUARES; 98" x 98"; white, black scrap; cotton & cotton blends; made in Louisiana in 1990; machine pieced, hand quilted; traditional polyfil. $690.00

6190691 – WINDY NURSERY RHYMES; 66" x 78"; seafoam green & rose; pre-washed cotton & polyester/cotton; made in Kentucky; hand embroidered & quilted; polyester fiberfill. $317.00

7190691 – APPLIQUED BEAR QUILT OR WALLHANGING; 35" x 40"; green & blue gingham check with light brown bear appliqued on tan background; part polyester, part cotton; made in Arkansas in 1990; hand appliqued & quilted; polyester batting. $55.00

1010991

2010991

3010991

4010991

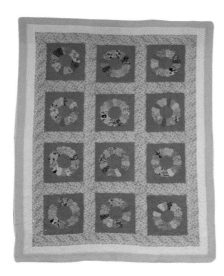

5010991

6010991

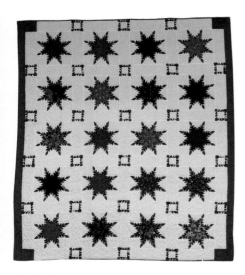

7010991

1010991 – TEPEE PEACE PIPE; 86" x 97"; earth tones with blue & green; cotton/polyester; made in Missouri in 1990; machine pieced, hand quilted; beige tepees camped in a circle, their doors opening to the village green, peace pipes cross on each point of star in the blue sky. $403.00

2010991 – COLOR CHAIN STAR; 92" x 99"; blue; cotton/polyester; made in Missouri in 1991; machine pieced, hand quilted; polyester batting. $403.00

3010991 – SQUARE IN A SQUARE; 86" x 101"; black & white; cotton/polyester; made in Missouri in 1991; machine pieced & quilted; polyester batting, black & white lining. $230.00

4010991 – BIBLICAL BLOCKS; 81" x 92"; mint green, red, white & black; cotton & cotton blends; made in Ohio in 1990; hand pieced, embroidered & quilted; 100% Traditional Polyester batting, one-piece lining, signed & dated. $690.00

5010991 – DRESDEN PLATE; 82" x 104"; white & yellow border, multicolored plate design with orange accent; 100% cotton; top made in Missouri in 1940 & finished in Iowa in 1988; old top hand & machine pieced, hand quilted; Mountain Mist batting. $317.00

6010991 – STAR IN ATTIC WINDOWS; 30" x 30"; navy blue, shades of purple, pinks, off-white; all cotton; made in Washington in 1988; hand pieced & quilted; low-loft poly batting, has rod pocket, initials & date embroidered on back. $92.00

7010991 – FEATHERED STAR; 89" x 102"; bright feathered stars with cream background; cotton-poly mix; made in Oregon in 1990; machine pieced, hand quilted; made from a Marsha McCloskey book. $345.00

117

1020991

2020991

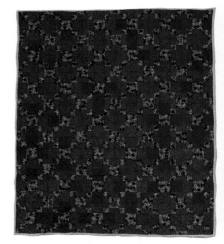

3020991

4020991

5020991

6020991

1020991 – FUN WITH DENIM; 64" x 64"; denim blue, red, white & green ribbons; denim, ribbon double face satin 100% polyester; made in Idaho in 1991; machine pieced, tied; ribbon put on by machine; bonded batting, binding doubled cotton, heavy quilt. $144.00

2020991 – POSTCARDS FROM MY SCRAP BOX; 34" x 50"; multicolored patches, black & white border, red binding, black, white & red back fabric; cottons, poly-cottons; made in Colorado in 1991; machine pieced, machine & hand quilted; Mountain Mist batting, has rod pocket, composed of post-card-size pieces of interesting fabrics, signed & dated. $190.00

3020991 – NINE PATCH VARIATION; 73" x 84"; blue, blue print, cream background; cotton with percale sheet for lining; made in Texas in 1990; machine pieced, hand quilted; Hobbs quilt batting, hand quilted with geometric design over the pieced design, lined & bound with a cream percale sheet, hand hemmed. $259.00

4020991 – HEARTS; 37" x 48"; baby blue pieced block on white background with small salmon heart appliqued in each block; poly & cotton; made in Arizona in 1990; machine pieced, hand appliqued & quilted; polyester batting. $55.00

5020991 – CRAZY QUILT; 33" x 35"; all colors, solids, stripes, brocades, back is blue moire with gold corduroy center strip; taffeta, satin, velvet, metallics; made in California in 1989; machine pieced, hand embroidered & tied; polyester batting, extra hand embroidery in several places. $115.00

6020991 – PLAIN SOLID; 43" x 63"; beige & peach; cotton polyester; made in Illinois in 1990; hand quilted; Dacron polyester batting, reversible, beige & peach lace. $60.00

7020991 – EMBROIDERED CIRCUS QUILT; 73" x 93"; yellow & blue with multicolored embroidery; cotton top, cotton/polyester backing; made in Kansas c. 1990; hand embroidery, blocks are machine pieced, hand quilted; light polyester batting, yellow fabric on back is lapped over to the front to form the binding. $230.00

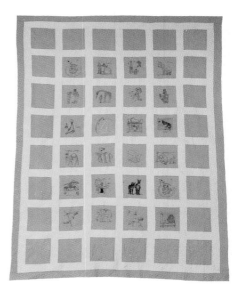

7020991

1030991

2030991

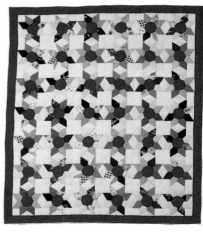

3030991

4030991

5030991

6030991

7030991

1030991 – NINE PATCH; 76" x 88"; brown print & unbleached muslin; all cotton; made in Mississippi in 1991; machine pieced, hand quilted; Fairfield polyester batting, unbleached muslin back, plain blocks have spiderweb quilting, pieced blocks are outline quilted. $345.00

2030991 – REARRANGED MISSOURI DAISY; 79" x 123"; royal blue pin-dot, pink flower centers, pink & blue flower patterned white; 100% cotton/cotton poly blends; made in Michigan in 1987; hand pieced & quilted; English piecing, washed once. $978.00

3030991 – FRIENDSHIP STAR; 80" x 92"; multicolored prints & solids; cotton & cotton blends; made in Arkansas in 1990; machine & hand pieced, hand quilted; polyester batting, stars are print & solid with solid blue broadcloth center, set together with muslin & design quilted in border & solid blue, quilted around each seam. $230.00

4030991 – TRIPLE IRISH CHAIN; 76" x 90"; multicolor set off with red & blue, white squares & back; cotton & cotton blends; made in Kansas in 1987; machine pieced, hand quilted; polyester batting, 5" multiprint border on 3 sides, large white squares quilted with large flower, remainder diagonal & crosshatch quilting. $460.00

5030991 – MOSAIC STAR; 88" x 97"; white, pink, maroon; cotton; made in Louisiana in 1988; machine pieced, hand quilted; polyester polyfill traditional batting, has 2 pillow shams. $547.00

6030991 – OLD FASHIONED NOSEGAY; 80" x 89"; multicolor prints set with beige; cotton & cotton blends; made in Ohio in 1987; hand pieced & quilted; Mountain Mist polyester batting, beige backing & binding, outline & design quilting in solid areas, signed & dated. $575.00

7030991 – BLUE CHIP WORRIES; 54" x 43"; blues, ivory ecru & tan; cotton blends; made in Pennsylvania in 1989; machine pieced, hand quilted; polyester batting, original design, signed. $259.00

119

1040991

2040991

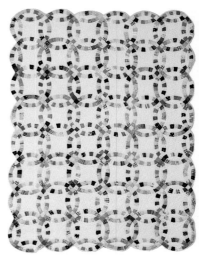

3040991

4040991

5040991

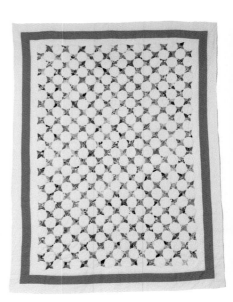

6040991

1040991 – AUTUMN OAKS (Oak Leaf Pattern); 78" x 95"; brown, beige & orange on muslin with brown lattices & borders; all cottons; made in Illinois in 1985; machine assembled, hand appliqued & quilted; Mountain Mist batting. $345.00

2040991 – PENN. STAR; 92" x 98"; blue; cotton/polyester; made in Missouri in 1990; machine pieced, hand quilted; 100% polyester batting. $403.00

3040991 – DOUBLE WEDDING RING; 78" x 105"; multicolor with cream background; cotton/polyester; made in Missouri in 1990; machine pieced, hand quilted; polyester batting. $345.00

4040991 – LOG CABIN; 6 ?" x 90"; blues, white, off-white, rust-red accent; cotton/cotton blend; made in Nebraska in 1991; machine pieced & quilted; polyfil batting. $156.00

5040991 – EMBROIDERED STAR; 80" x 93"; orchid & white; 50/50 poly cotton; made in Illinois in 1991; machine pieced, hand quilted; poly batting, bound with prairie points. $345.00

6040991 – 4 POINT STARS; 78" x 104"; multicolored star on white background with red border; 50% poly, 50% cotton; machine pieced, hand quilted; top is approximately 30 to 40 years old, border was added & quilted in 1990, Mountain Mist batting. $317.00

7040991 – PINWHEEL; 72" x 96"; blue & white; cotton; made in Kentucky in 1991; machine pieced, hand quilted; Mountain Mist batting, pre-washed material, outline quilting of pinwheel hearts in plain blocks. $345.00

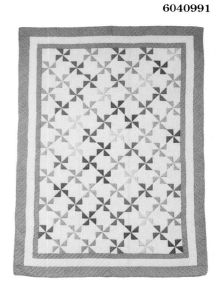

7040991

1050991

2050991

3050991

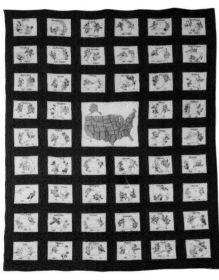

4050991

5050991

6050991

7050991

1050991 – MY FLOWER GARDEN; 83" x 96"; pale yellow background with various colors of flowers; cotton/blends; made in Kansas in 1979; hand appliqued & quilted; polyester bonded batting, every other block is quilted in water lily design, picot edging, includes matching wallhanging. $460.00

2050991 – GIANT DAHLIA; 76" x 96"; pinks, green, prints on off-white background; 100% cotton; made in Florida in 1989; machine pieced, hand quilted; Mountain Mist low loft batting, feather scroll quilting with diagonal background quilting. $460.00

3050991 – BEAR PAW; 80" x 97"; blue, white; cotton; made in New Mexico in 1990; machine pieced & quilted; Mountain Mist batting. $288.00

4050991 – STATE QUILT; 85" x 105"; multicolor embroidered birds & flowers with brown borders & white backing; poly & cotton; made in South Dakota in 1989; machine pieced, hand embroidered & appliqued; poly batting, embroidered in multicolors of birds & feathers with lots of hand quilting & fancy stitched embroidery. $1,610.00

5050991 – THE LOVE QUILT; 79" x 91"; multicolor set together with whie, edging & backing are country blue pin-dot; poly/cotton, calico; made in Arizona in 1990; machine & hand pieced, hand quilted, yellow centers appliqued; Mountain Mist batting, double quilted. $460.00

6050991 – OHIO STAR; 86" x 100"; burgundy & white; cotton; made in Texas in 1991; machine pieced, hand quilted; feather wreath in plain blocks. $374.00

7050991 – LOVER'S KNOT; 66" x 100"; aqua, mauve & white; cotton & cotton blends; made in Nebraska in 1990; machine pieced, hand quilted; polyfil batting. $259.00

1060991

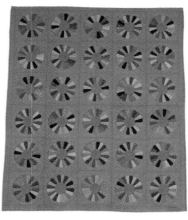

2060991

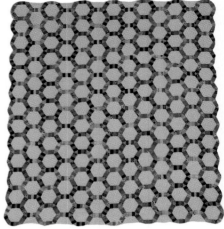

3060991

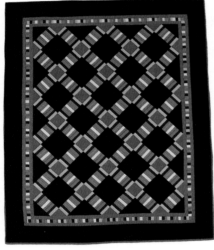

4060991

5060991

6060991

1060991 – ANIMAL TREE; 40½" x 50"; greens, browns & primary colors with muslin background; 100% cotton; made in Arkansas in 1991; hand appliqued, embroidered & quilted; polyfil thin batting, outline quilting & small clamshell in background, embellished with beaded eyes on "creatures," 100% cotton back & handmade bias binding, rod pocket, signed & dated. $144.00

2060691 – POINTED DRESDEN PLATES; 78" x 94"; multi pastel prints on aqua print background with white backing; made in Virginia in 1990; hand & machine pieced, hand appliqued & quilted; 100% cottons; traditional poly bonded batting, heavily quilted, original designs, double bias bound with mitered corners, signed & dated. $633.00

3060691 – FRIENDSHIP RING; 80" x 89"; various prints & solids on white background; cotton & cotton blends; made in Arkansas in 1990; hand pieced & quilted; polyester batting, double bias binding. $259.00

4060691 – RAILROAD CROSSING; 84" x 105"; Amish colors on black with blue border & backing; 100% prewashed cotton; made in Illinois in 1991; machine pieced, hand quilted; popular Ohio Amish pattern, Putnam batting. $547.00

5060691 – VARIABLE STAR; 86" x 104"; bold Amish colors on black with black background; 100% prewashed cotton; made in Illinois in 1991; machine pieced, hand quilted; black Putnam batting. $575.00

6060691 – RAIL FENCE VARIATION; 90" x 102"; blue & rose; cotton; made in Oregon in 1989; machine pieced & quilted. $311.00

7060691 – TRIP AROUND THE WORLD; 84" x 102"; blue & white; cottons; made in Pennsylvania in 1990; machine pieced, hand quilted; bonded polyester batting, double binding. $403.00

7060991

1070991

2070991

3070991

4070691

5070691

6070691

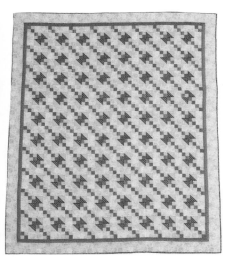

7070991

1070991 – BROKEN STAR; 28" x 28"; black, peach, blue; all cotton; made in South Carolina in 1990; machine pieced, hand quilted; Mountain Mist batting. $110.00

2070991 – PENNSYLVANIA DUTCH; 76" x 88"; rose with multicolored stars; cotton; made c. 1900; hand pieced & quilted; light cotton batting, 2 stars worn but graphic design beautiful. $345.00

3070991 – GRANDMOTHER'S FANCY; 79" x 86"; assorted; old time cottons; made in Delaware in 1970's; hand pieced & quilted. $200.00

4070991 – COUNTRY CLASSIC; 87" x 87"; pink & blue; cotton; made in Oklahoma in 1990; machine pieced, hand quilted; cotton-poly blend batting. $575.00

5070991 – SOLID – PLAIN; 92" x 106"; unbleached muslin/blue; cotton polyester; made in Illinois in 1991; hand made, hand quilted; Dacron poly batting, reversible (blue side is shown). $230.00

6070991 – SAMPLER; 86" x 89"; multicolor; cotton. $115.00

7070991 – HEARTS CONTENT; 84" x 100"; pink, rose, seafoam green; 100% prewashed cottons; made in Colorado in 1991; machine pieced, hand quilted; poly batting, quilted with lots of hearts, signed & dated. $690.00

1080991

2080991

3080991

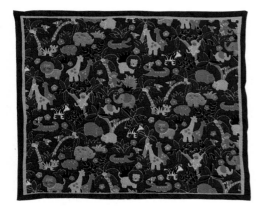

4080691

5080691

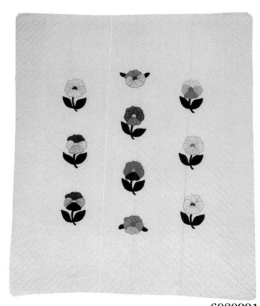

6080991

7080691

1080991 – TRIP AROUND THE WORLD; 105" x 105"; various prints; polyester cotton; made in Tennessee in 1987; machine pieced, hand quilted; polyester batting. $288.00

2080991 – SCOTTYS; 36" x 50"; blue tartan plaid, yellow sashing; made in Oregon in 1991; machine pieced, hand tied; prewashed fabric. $50.00

3080991 – LOG CABIN (Barn Raising Setting); 73" x 98"; blues, rose & tans; 100% cotton; made in Ohio in 1988; machine pieced, hand quilted; Fairfield Traditional batting, quilted in the ditch in log cabin blocks, line quilting in border, signed & dated. $230.00

4080991 – MY JUNGLE BUDDIES; 45" x 39"; red, blue, green, yellow; cotton blend; made in 1991; hand quilted around each animal; polyester batting. $100.00

5080991 – KING'S CROWN; 16" x 47"; green, red & off-white background; cotton; made in Florida in 1988; machine pieced, hand quilted & appliqued; Mountain Mist light batting, off-white muslin backing bound in green paisley. $92.00

6080991 – PANSY; 88" x 108"; multicolored with white background; cotton & polyester; made in Kansas in 1991; hand quilted & appliqued; each pansy is a different color combination, polyfil, sheet lining. $345.00

7080991 – DREAM FLIGHT; 49" x 65"; bright multicolors with light blue background; cotton/shiny cotton; made in Kentucky in 1989; hand quilted, applique technique, some embroidery; poly batting, original design of hot air balloons with colored circles representing clouds & a fabric print to represent trees, has borders that represent hot air balloons. $690.00

1090991

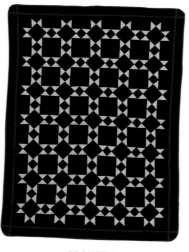

2090991

3090991

4090991

5090991

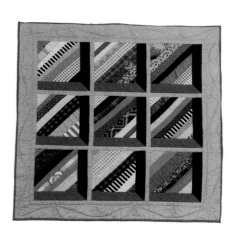

6090991

7090991

1090991 – FAN MEDALLION; 84" x 101"; blues, burgundys & mauves background; 100% cotton; made in Indiana in 1990; machine pieced & quilted; Fairfield Traditional batting, fans are assembled in random scrap patchwork of coordinated fabrics & a secondary pattern is formed using the Irish Cross-roads block. $299.00

2090991 – EVENING STAR; 51" x 68"; black background with cream colored stars & green border; 100% cotton; made in Georgia in 1990; machine pieced, hand quilted; Polyfil Traditional batting, has rod pocket. $230.00

3090991 – WEDDING RING; 78" x 89"; wine print on white; cotton; made in Illinois in 1991; machine pieced, hand quilted; polyester batting. $276.00

4090991 – DOUBLE IRISH CHAIN; 88" x 89"; lavender, blue & white; cotton; made in Wisconsin in 1990; machine pieced & quilted; poly batting, quilted with rose motif. $288.00

5090991 – DANCING DAFFODILS; 80" x 101"; light cream, 3 values of soft rose; 100% cotton; made in Ohio in 1991; hand quilted; polyester batting, blind stitched appliqued, hand quilted with patterns of shell, chain & intricate flowers – daffodils, leaves & stems are swaying curves, double binding. $547.00

6090991 – ATTIC WINDOW; 42" x 42¼"; light blue & purples with multicolor view; cottons, polished cotton; made in Colorado in 1991; machine pieced, machine & hand quilted; Mountain Mist polyester batting. $259.00

7090991 – CHRISTMAS FEATHERED STAR; 30" x 30"; red, green, off-white; cotton, cotton polyester; made in Minnesota in 1990; hand pieced & quilted; polyester batting, has rod pocket, feather & cable quilting designs, signed & dated. $144.00

1100691

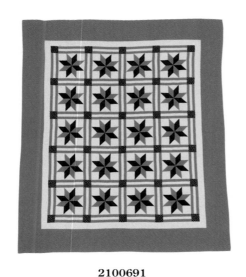

2100691

3100691

4100691

5100691

6100691

1100691 – SISTER'S STAR; 83" x 102"; off-white, peach, green; 100% cotton; made in New York in 1991; machine pieced & quilted; polyester batting, free-motion machine quilting gives hand quilted look, flowers in white blocks & trailing floral vine in borders. $403.00

2100691 – 8 POINT STAR; 79" x 84"; red, white & blue; cotton & cotton/poly; made in Florida; machine pieced, hand quilted; Mountain Mist batting. $460.00

3100691 – CHRISTMAS LONE STAR; 49" x 46"; Christmas prints; cotton; machine pieced, hand quilted; polyester batting, solid dark green background, top & bottom are bordered with pieced red diamonds, red print border, bound in white with white backing, peace doves are quilted with white thread & on all four sides of diamonds. $288.00

4100691 – BLUE LOG CABIN; 30" x 30"; blue scraps, muslin; cotton & blends; made in North Carolina in 1991; machine pieced & quilted; Cotton Classic batting, quilted in the ditch & radiating lines, blue print on backing. $110.00

5100691 – SAILBOATS; 45" x 58"; royal blue, red, white; cotton, poly cotton; made in Wisconsin in 1991; machine pieced, hand & machine quilted, hand & machine appliqued, hand embroidered; 100% bonded polyester batting, sails are four different patterns. $110.00

6100691 – MEMORIES OF HAWAII; 82" x 82"; dark blue & green on light blue with solid blue backing; cotton; made in New Jersey in 1990; hand appliqued & quilted; poly batting. $978.00

7100691 – MISSOURI PUZZLE; 30" x 31"; black & white; cotton polyester; made in Missouri in 1990; machine pieced & quilted; Dacron batting, black & white solids & prints, black lining, loops for wallhanging. $70.00

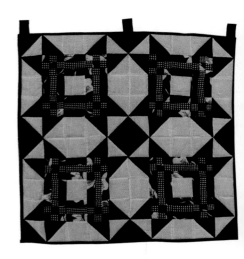

7100691

1120991

2120991

3120991

4120991

5120991

6120991

7120991

1120991 – CHRISTMAS STAR; 23" x 23"; red, green, white; cotton; made in North Carolina in 1984; machine pieced, hand & machine quilted; polyester batting, holly design quilted in 5 of white blocks, gold pin-dot in red & green fabric. $100.00

2120991 – FLOWERS ON A VINE; 84" x 96"; blue, red, red print & green leaves & vines on white background; made in Indiana in 1991, hand appliqued & quilted; polyester batting. $1,035.00

3120991 – TREE OF LIFE; 86" x 96"; white, blue, red, orange, yellow & green; percale & cotton blend; made in Indiana in 1990; hand made; polyester batting. $1,495.00

4120991 – COBBLESTONES; 76" x 84"; variegated prints, plaids, etc.; cottons & poly cotton blends; made in Kentucky in 1989; hand & machine pieced, machine quilted. $173.00

5120991 – HILLBILLIES; 72" x 90"; white with amber sashes; 50/50 blends; made in Kentucky in 1990; hand painted, machine quilted white lining; polyester batting, brown check binding. $230.00

6120991 – DOUBLE IRISH CHAIN WITH HEARTS; 82" x 103"; rose, gray & white with rose pin-dot background; cotton pin-dot & floral prints; made in Connecticut in 1991; machine piece, hand quilted; polyester batting, hearts appliqued onto background blocks, quilted in crosshatching with folk-art design around hearts and tulip & swag design quilted in border area, double bias bound edges, signed & dated. $460.00

7120991 – BABY BLOCKS; 65" x 90"; brown print & dusty rose (plain & print); cotton; made in Illinois in 1989; machine pieced, hand quilted; polyester batting. $288.00

The AMERICAN Quilter's Society

Invites You To Become A Member Today!

You will receive quarterly issues of *American Quilter* magazine plus all of these other benefits for only $15.00 for your one-year membership. Your savings on one AQS book order will probably be more than this low membership fee.

In order to become a member of the American Quilter's Society, send your check or charge card information. You will receive your membership pin and card by return mail.

ORDER TOLL-FREE WHEN USING VISA OR MASTERCARD (1-800-626-5420)

Museum Of The American Quilter's Society

We invite you to Paducah, Kentucky for the quilt experience of your life!
See three galleries of priceless quilts, including the MAQS Permanent Collection, which includes quilts that have won Best-Of-Show and Workmanship Awards in past AQS National Shows.
There is a gift shop, and workshops are offered. Contact MAQS for more information:

MAQS • 215 Jefferson Street • Paducah, KY 42001 • (502) 442-8856

Membership Pin

An elegant maroon and gold pin signifies that you have had the vision to join the American Quilter's Society to help promote the art of quilting and set the standard of excellence that all who love quilting desire to achieve.

Savings On Quilting Books

Periodically you will receive a list of many books on quilting. As a member, you can buy any of these books at attractive savings.

American Quilter's Society
P. O. Box 3290 • Dept B • Paducah, KY 42002-3290

National Quilt Show

Free admission for members. Each spring in Paducah, Kentucky, 400 exquisite quilts are displayed with more than $70,000 in cash awards. Workshops, lectures, authors, fashion show and Merchants Mall are also featured.

Quilts For Sale Service

We are offering our members the opportunity to have quilts they would like to sell photographed and listed in a catalog at no expense to members.

AMERICAN QUILTER Magazine

This beautiful, colorful magazine is exclusively for members of AQS. It is not available to the public or on newsstands. Spring, Summer, Fall, and Winter issues are sent to you free. As a member, you can share your experiences, techniques and beautiful creations and promote your accomplishments through this magazine.